ENDORSEMENTS

This Is Your Chance, by Timothy McCain will remove the blinders of self-doubt and petty excuses from the eyes of your destiny. This is not another motivational message that leaves you empty and envious of others' success, but rather equips you to embrace your purpose. Read this with anticipation and expectation that your "next" is right around the corner!

- Jamie Jones,
Lead Pastor of Trinity Church,
Author of "The Left-Handed Warrior"

I have always subscribed to the phrase "Bodies in motion tend to stay in motion." More often than not, we *wander* into victory rather than *wonder* into success. Many of us struggle with taking the first of many steps toward an amazing life we have often wondered about. Wait and wonder no more! This book by Timothy McCain will awaken the pioneer that has been taken prisoner by unruly mentalities and habits. You will rise and walk into your greatest life as you read and apply Rev. McCain's principles.

—Evangelist Allen Griffin
Author of "Undefeated"

Timothy brings practical and direct steps on how to engage the opportunities that are in front of us. If you dare to chase down your dreams and live out your full potential, you must get your hands on this book.

-Jamey Paugh
President of Paugh International

Timothy McCain is challenging men and women to step into their purpose in "This is Your Chance." His desire for a fully functioning church is the impetus for this book that will encourage you to take action, move past fear, and step into more. Take the challenge and make it happen!

John Ryan Cantu
Pastor of Primera Iglesia in Houston TX
Host of Leading: The Christian Leadership Podcast

"This Is Your Chance" is a practical approach to powerful results. Timothy break downs the fundamentals of achieving goals that we often have dreamed about, but never put steps in place. I appreciate his healthy approach towards life and you will see it shine through in this book. At the end of this book I believe you will feel encouraged to chase after the dreams God has given you and that God has equipped you perfectly for it.

-Nate Ortiz
Ohio District Youth Director

THIS
IS
YOUR
CHANCE

TIMOTHY MCCAIN

THIS
IS
YOUR
CHANCE

IT'S NOT OPPORTUNITY THAT WILL PASS YOU BY;
IT'S MORE LIKE YOU WILL PASS BY
YOUR OPPORTUNITY

Xulon Press
2301 Lucien Way #415
Maitland, FL 32751
407.339.4217
www.xulonpress.com

Printed in the United States of America.

ISBN-13: 978-1-5456-7592-2

DEDICATION

I dedicate this book to my wife and son. Y'all are the reason why I wake up early and go to bed late. Y'all are my reasons and my motivations. Madai and Hezekiah, I love y'all and am glad I get the honor to call y'all family.

In memory of Wil Hernandez

TABLE OF CONTENTS

ACKNOWLEDGMENTS

My wife, Madai, and son, Hezekiah
My family and friends
Trinity Church family in Deltona, FL
The Movement Young Adults
First Assembly of God, Fort Wayne, IN
First Assembly of God Asheboro, NC
North Carolina Masters Commission
River of Life Church International
Pastors Jamie & Michelle Jones
Trinity Church Staff
Bishop Tony and Kathy Miller
Evangelists Allen and Hashmareen Griffin
Evangelists Jamey and Amber Paugh
Evangelists Pat and Karen Schatzline
Pastors Don and Nancy Williams
Pastors John and Melissa Cantu
Pastors Matt and Sydney Hammersky
Pastor Nate Ortiz
Amy Pratt
Pablo and Liz Abreu
Singer Family
Stensland Family
Revilla Family
Choi Family

INTRODUCTION

I believe that there is a purpose, calling and destiny for the life of everyone walking the earth today. However, there are many people living frustrated and in disappointment due to the lack of fulfillment. It may be easy to stand on a soap box and blame someone else for your current state, but consider that the greatest hurdle to climb over is the one staring back at you in the mirror. Yes, there are major mountains that need to be overcome, but it is also the small but potent mindsets that we have that imprison us in uncertainty.

Do you find yourself saying, "One day I am going to start my business, go back to school or write a book?" Are you putting your goals in the distance, waiting for things to just happen, when the things that need to happen are waiting on you? Procrastination, insecurities, and fears are just a few characteristics that halt your purpose. Yet, I assure you the reasons go even deeper than that to a well of excuses disguised as reasons. Do you find yourself saying "I can't" to challenges when in reality you really mean "I won't"? Have you given difficulty and impossibility the same definition, thus giving yourself permission not to try at all?

You owe it to yourself to take an in-depth journey in your life and confront the monsters roaring in the closet of your mind. Monsters of laziness, feeling inadequate, and the negative voices both within and around you. This is your chance to turn things around, to see yourself the way God sees you.

One of my family's favorite shows is a show on HGTV called "Fixer Upper." It is a home improvement makeover show that uses the worst house in the best neighborhood and creates something special. It stars a couple named Chip and Joanna Gaines, and they are extremely gifted in what they do. But what brings me back to the show is not simply the end results, but the process it takes to get there.

Every episode starts the same way as the host takes clients who are looking to purchase a home to see some houses in their price range. Mind you, that these homes aren't nice looking homes at all. Some homes just need cosmetic touch ups and a makeover. While others demanded more work and are rundown, broken, water damaged, and for some, unlivable. For many people it is the home that people will drive by and never would have thought to live in. The expression on the clients' faces when they pull up to the home is priceless. They look at each other while making statements such as, "This is ugly," or "I can't live here." Chip and Joanna stand with them in the front yard and confirm with them that the house is ugly, broken down, and maybe has been neglected. Chip describes the square footage, the year it was built and other details, but many times people aren't moved by facts alone because they can't seem to get past what they see right before their eyes.

Finally, they go into the house and at first it seems to take a nose-dive as the inside can look worse than the outside. Broken glass, horrible paint, small rooms and tight corners. At first they can't imagine themselves living in that home, and are very vocal about it. They tell them all the reasons why this would never work out.

However, next is the reason why I come back to the show over and over again. Joanna starts to share what she sees and envisions for the house. She tells them that they can knock down a wall here, add hard flooring there, remodel the kitchen and other radical changes. And while she is describing its modifications to them, all of a sudden, the clients' expressions change. Instead of shaking their head no, they are nodding yes. They are getting ahold of the vision of what is possible even without anything changing around them. There wasn't new paint on the walls, lights in the kitchen or a remodeled living room. Nothing changed around them, but something did shift within them. They saw the possibilities for the house that they were standing in and later purchased the house. Every episode we see the process needed to take place as things didn't change in a day. They discovered issues along the way, problems that they didn't know about, but they had to overcome them to present the new home to the couple. It went from being the worst house in the best neighborhood to one of the best homes in the neighborhood.

Your Fixer Upper

Maybe you feel that your life has areas that are impossible to fix. Maybe you believe that the dreams, goals and desires inside of you will never come to pass. Do you look in the mirror and believe that you are the worst house in the best neighborhood? Have you and others discounted you because you don't have the same giftings, upbringing, or funds as other people? Are you a fixer upper?

The feeling of inadequacy causes many people to live beneath their purpose. We forfeit chances and moments to be the best version of ourselves. Yet it is oftentimes because of the subtle excuses or adopted reasoning that we will delay our own breakthrough. Laziness, insecurities, fear or when we say "I can't" when we really mean "I won't" are wrenches thrown into the plan God has for our lives. Make up in your mind that you aren't going to waste another day living in fear and anxiety. This is your moment to no longer simply be a daydreamer but a day-doer. This is your chance to start your business, go back to college or whatever those aspirations may be. Fear has kept you in prison long enough. God has an appointment for you and a destiny that you must not miss. Actually, He is calling your number right now, so gather your things, stand up and take the leap towards your purpose. This is your chance.

CHAPTER 1
WHY NOT ME?

Opportunity is an unseized responsibility. Responsibility is just ownership of opportunity. I believe many people are not living up to their full potential because they are not taking ownership of the opportunity around them. Potential is the precursor and seed of opportunity, while responsibility is the byproduct of the opportunity; thus, the achievement is the harvest of responsibility. Therefore, if you do not appreciate the seed, you will never eat the fruit. With this in mind, it is not really opportunity that will pass you by, but more like you will walk past opportunity. It is imperative that you know without a shadow of a doubt that this is your chance.

Have you ever been lying down on a relaxing evening, scrolling through Instagram, clicking on stories, seeing the amazing lives other people are living? Maybe it is the entrepreneur that is traveling every other week to a different country using hashtags like #LivingMyBestLife. They will talk about how they can do this because of the passive income they have built through the years and how you can do it too. Have you ever seen a post like that, and the first thing you thought was that it was fake and impossible? Another swipe up with your thumb, and an image of a fitness model appeared, showing a before and after picture. The picture on the left was showing an overweight picture of themselves, binge eating and drinking at a party. The picture on the right was now showing them

3

drinking a protein shake with ripped abs, chiseled quads, and massive biceps. Below the picture, they write out a detailed description of their diet and workout regimen, laying out the steps they took to turn their life around.

Photoshop in and of itself is not bad at all. It is fun and hilarious to see some of the unique videos, graphics, and photos they have created. In your mind, you see the picture and think, "That is unrealistic, it's impossible, it's Photoshopped." It is a dangerous mindset to have, that we view success and results as out of reach. We give ourselves permission to not act on our desires through an apathetic attitude towards life. For many reasons, we can have more hope for a stranger's success, yet look within ourselves and feel inadequate even to dream. Thus, choosing to live the nightmare that we create every day by living without ambitions or aspirations. I understand that everything you see on social media isn't real; a level of skepticism is healthy. However, if we write off everything as unrealistic, we will give ourselves permission to keep swiping and never living. Due to the ability that Photoshop has to create an image that isn't true, we have been groomed to question what we see. People are flexing their proverbial muscle, showing off cars that they don't own, bodies that they didn't build, and money they didn't earn — highlighting the best times with their families when they are getting along, yet not posting the times when infighting is happening.

The dynamic of social media demands a level of suspicion, so you don't get manipulated into chasing imaginary realities. The vulnerability we have created due to Photoshop is that we have been wired to question results; thus, we never try. The first thing we think about is how something is unachievable, so why try? However, we must not become cynical, to create a mindset that good times, happiness, and fortune are unattainable. With a Photoshop mindset, it isn't seeing that is believing but the experience that makes one believe. However, the most challenging step to take, to see if something is true, is the first step out of complacency. It is the fatigued steps of hope that drag if letdown and defeat have worn them out.

Could we have been allowing our history and legacy to pass us by on a daily basis because we can't see opportunity? Have we been waiting for an opportunity to ring our doorbells while we sit on our couches of laziness, debating if it is worth getting up to see what it has to offer? Living like this is an unfulfilling way to live.

It is looking at the lives of others, believing that the reason why they are the way they are is solely because they are special or got lucky. To solely believe that it is luck discounts their grind, hustle, sacrifice, and consistency that they sowed into the unknown and obscure seasons of their lives. It is looking at the fruit of their labor, but not staring at the tree which allows a harvest in the first place.

Success didn't just arrive at their door. No, they had to run there themselves. They were the Uber eats, making trips to serve their future with orders of "I don't quit" and self-motivation. It's not really opportunity that will pass you by, but more like you will walk past opportunity. I am not speaking from a place of theory but of experience. I thought that success was on the table for everyone else, and I was eating three square meals of insecurities. But I remember when I finally made

> It's not really opportunity that will pass you by, but more like you will walk past opportunity.

a choice to push the plate aside and cook for myself. I can recall as if it was yesterday when I took my chance. I yelled within a war cry that birthed a drive in me that I didn't know existed. The faith that I preached all around the world grew even deeper roots as I chose to give it all I had.

Three simple words challenged my way of thinking, and completely changed my life: WHY NOT ME?

Dyslexia

I grew up thinking that I was flat out stupid. Not just uneducated, but that I had no ability even to gain, to learn, grow, and blossom like other people around me. I am a silent, keep-to-myself kind of man, and I spend a lot of time thinking. So many times, I would be in deep thought, dreaming about how different my life would be if I could do the same things as other people. But I was broken, useless and dumb, or at least I thought I was. Yet, there would be so many people around me who would say that I was smart and wise beyond my age, and I just assumed that they were being nice.

A pastor named Don Williams was one of those consistent voices, telling me these words I so badly wanted to take root in my mind, but I truly believed that it was impossible. Now every time I see him, I thank him for being a verbal farmer who cast seeds of hope in me even when I thought I would never see a harvest. I grew up in a little city in North Carolina with a large family. One thing that blessed me then and is blessing me so much today is to see other people succeed and thrive. Watching my siblings succeed and thrive brings me joy. They are all doing very well in many different walks of life.

From a young age, I saw how bright and talented they were, and I knew they would be extremely successful. But when I looked in the mirror, I didn't see the same bright future ahead of me, but a flickering flame of hope barely staying lit. When I was in elementary school, I had to take speech classes due to issues with a slur and stutter. When I was in middle school, I had to go through testing for my reading because I had a hard time retaining information. I would read a paragraph, and when I was asked to tell them what it was about, I couldn't recall the story. From my youngest memory, I truly believed that I was stupid, and I had no idea what future was in store. If an opportunity was going to pass by, I just knew it was going to skip my address. When I would write and discover a word I couldn't spell, I would have to erase the entire sentence. I would then have to reword the sentence with a word that I knew how to spell. It was frustrating, to say the least, and this was a prison that I kept myself in for so long.

When I was getting closer to my senior year, I had no idea what I wanted to do with my life. Beyond that, I had zero ideas as to what I was qualified to become. I made a choice to take steps to go into the Army and even went to take my ASVAB test to be allowed to join. Yet I received another punch to the gut that I thought highlighted my own issues: I failed the test horribly. For over thirty years, I felt utterly dumb. I believed that my dyslexia was getting the best of me, and I couldn't overcome it. I firmly believed that I was hopeless, and my future wasn't bright but dim, a nightmare from which I would never wake up.

Why Not ME?

But from the most random source possible, I experienced a life-altering and mind-shifting encounter that was the epiphany I had been waiting for since my younger days. I was scrolling through Instagram, and I saw a post with a quote from Albert Einstein along with a cartoon drawing. The picture was of a few different animals positioned side by side. There was a bird, monkey, penguin, elephant, a fish in a bowl, a seal and a dog. Behind the animals was a huge tree, which helped to create the tone of the picture. In front of the animals was a man seated behind a desk, saying: "For a fair selection everybody has to take the same exam: Please climb that tree." Below the artwork were the words of a quote by Albert Einstein, whom I would later discover had dyslexia. "Everybody is a genius, but if you judge a fish by its ability to climb a tree, it will live its whole life believing that it is stupid."

This rocked me to the core, and it was like a switch had been flipped inside me. Like I had a near-death experience, I had a new appreciation about life and its possibilities. For the first time, I didn't see myself as a stupid man with no future and absent of hope. I told myself, "All this time I was upset because I had a hard time mentally climbing the tree, but what if I was meant to soar above it?" I started to see myself in an entirely new way, and looked into my future with fresh vision and fresh expectations. It was like I was born for the third time in my life. The first on September 30, 1986, when I was born, and the second time was when I gave my life to Jesus and was born again. But at this moment, through a simple yet profound post, I was reborn and awakened to the possibilities before me. I am not dumb, and I am not stupid, my giftings are just different, not obsolete.

It was like the moment that Jesus had been waiting for and preparing me to have. I started to see myself in the same way that He saw me, in the humblest extent that could be. I didn't see myself as an oops, mistake, or an accident. I no longer believed that I was limited, but there were unlimited possibilities waiting for me. Finally, my eyes were open to opportunity in and of itself. I felt a fire in my bones and dreams boiling within me. Like an avalanche sweeping over every excuse, I told myself that I was going to make up for all the time that I had wasted, living beneath my purpose. I knew without a shadow of a doubt that this was my chance.

I was scrolling through social media and saw a short clip from an interview with Pastor Steven Furtick and Bishop T.D Jakes about this book called *Soar.* It was just a short clip of Bishop T.D Jakes talking about at a time in ministry that he felt like quitting. It was so powerful and ministered to me so deeply, I immediately went to YouTube and watched the entire influential interview. It was as if every word was a thread and needle sewing up the holes in my life. The voices of insecurities that I would have allowed to tell me that this wasn't for me were silenced. I had zero patience to order the book online, so I went to my nearest Walmart late one night and picked up the book. I was hungry to start living out my purpose. I was desperate to finally stop giving myself permission to live under the lies of "I won't" masquerading as "I can't."

Bishop Jakes book *Soar,* inspired me tremendously, and equipped me along the way. It is a practical book about entrepreneurship and business, and gives practical tools to shift from theory to reality. I have a very strong conviction to be a man of my word. I want my yes to be yes, and my no to be no. When I make a commitment to someone, I go out of my way to make sure it happens. I realized that I gave everyone else that level of commitment, but not myself. I made a commitment to myself to go to college and get a business degree, start my own business, and write my first book. I discovered an entrepreneur niche YouTube channel that I gleaned from, called Valuetainment, led by Patrick Bet-David. I was a sponge as I learned from the information shared on the channel. I started a YouTube channel called "TMMotivations," and I have the goal to speak in schools, to governments, and different arenas all around the world.

In the span of a few short months, I started college at an amazing school called Nyack College, pursuing a business degree and started my own business; an LLC called TMM. Around that time, I wrote my first book, over 64,000 words, called *Crowns Are Greater Than Trophies.* I am aware that there is a risk of this coming across as bragging, but I assure you it is not. This is a testament to the fact of how radically your life can change if you dare to start, if you dare to recognize that this is your chance. The entire time I was writing the book, studying for tests and taking exams, I would repeat the same simple three words that marked a season in my life: **Why not me?** I had to make sure that I didn't allow frustration to become a bellboy carrying the baggage of my past into my future.

It is remarkable, the power that the blend of believing God at His word and believing in yourself can manifest. I used to place furthering my education at the furthest point from my mind, but I was amazed that I was making A's in my courses. The first semester was over, and I had a 3.5 GPA average, and even at the time of the writing of this book, I have kept the average. Fear is the biggest liar in the room and gives birth to the greatest regrets. For over thirty years of my life, I pushed my purpose aside and didn't seize the opportunities around me. But after the encounter on Instagram and life-altering encounter viewing Pastor Steven Furtick, the Bishop T.D Jakes interview, and Patrick Bet-David YouTube channel, I was motivated to turn my life around. I watched the same *Soar* interview almost every day and listened to Valuetainment while repeating the same words: **Why not me?**

Opportunity

Opportunity doesn't pass us by. We are the ones who walk past it. It is hard to see sometimes because we may not be looking for it. A possibility we aren't looking for because we don't believe we are ready for it in the first place. When you are walking through the grocery store, there are all sorts of food everywhere. When my wife sends me to the store, I have learned to ask for an exact list of the items she needs or wants. If not, I spend my time in an area I don't need to be in and waste our money on items we don't even need. But in that store, if I knew where to look and had the skills to cook, I could prepare any meal you could think of. Have you ever been in a place in life where you have a longing for a specific meal, but you have no idea how to prepare it? You walk through the store wondering, "Do I need this item or not?" Have you ever had a taste for greatness and to live out your purpose, but had no idea how to prepare the meal to consume it? There are directions to cook any meal in a cookbook, but we must be responsible enough to use the tool in the first place.

Responsibility

If you are going to cook that fantastic meal, then you are responsible for seeking out the steps to prepare it — a cookbook is full of recipes that take seemingly random items and create gourmet dishes. The eggs aren't just going to jump into your cart, and the butter isn't just going to appear. After you discover what you need, you must reach out and take it. Waiting for the opportunity to transform into a tangible and obtainable result is insanity. We are required to make an effort to gather the tools we need to reach our goals. In order to shift from an aspiring person full of ideas but never any follow-up, you must take action. Hail down the taxi of opportunity and view it as your duty to be responsible enough to ride it from the feeling of being insignificant over the bridge of determination. Follow the instructions in the recipe book and feast on the fruit of your labors. There is no more time to waste and no more excuses to give. Your family, business, legacy, dreams, and goals are walking on the other side of your "yes." What you are envisioning may seem silly to others, but this isn't a childhood game of "red light, green light." You don't stop moving forward and kill your tempo just because someone yells out "stop." This is your chance and the time is now.

Overlooked Masterpiece

To this day, people all around the world celebrate the artistic masterpieces of Michelangelo's art. One of his most famous sculptures is the statue of David, which was created out of a single block of marble. The journey to make the statue didn't just start at the young age of twenty-six when he started it, but over a century before that. It is said that the massive block of marble sat untouched for over 100 years. An artist obtained the stone but didn't have a purpose for it at the time. If only the stone could have spoken as it sat untouched and unused. If it had feelings, would it have wondered when it was its turn to be transformed? Maybe it would have thought, after the years passed by that becoming a masterpiece just wasn't in the cards it was dealt.

Michelangelo would later come across the block of marble and have a vision for it. It is a powerful notion to know that purpose flows from the veins of vision. When one artist had no vision, the marble sat without a purpose. But when an artist had a vision or something was cast aside, it officially became set apart. Between 1501 and 1504, the statue of David was created, an amazing masterpiece. Many people admired Michelangelo's work and rightly so, as it was and still is incredible. He would later be asked a question of how he created the statue of David, and his response was remarkable.

"The sculpture is already complete within the marble block, before I start my work. It is already there, I just have to chisel away the superfluous material." — Michelangelo Buonarroti

There is a masterpiece inside of you, and it is longing to appear before you. There is a legacy that is connected to your name that demands you stop wasting time and seize your opportunities by the horns. Maybe, like the statue, you sat untouched and unmoved for years. Maybe you started to believe a lie that you missed your moment and the time was too late. If you did, then I am glad to inform you that you are wrong. The Lord has a hammer in His hand, and He is handing you a chisel. There is greatness inside of you, and He is tearing down the excuses, fears, doubts, and other paralyzing thoughts that are nailing your feet to the ground. So why not you?

Grab your hard hat and your work boots because you have entered your construction zone. It is time to work, and you will break a sweat building your dreams and goals. This is your chance!

CHAPTER 2
FIFTY-TWO MONDAYS

If only I had more money, then I could do it.

I'm not smart enough, so why should I even try?

The last time I tried, it didn't work out, so what is the point of trying again?

Well, if I had it as easy as them, then I could do it too.

Everyone keeps telling me that I can't do it and maybe they are right.

Do these phrases and words sound familiar? Have they been the fruit that you have been consuming from the verbal seeds that have harvested in your mind? Have you heard negativity enough that you changed your address from faith to fear, and established your residence in that culture of uncertainty? Have you ever been in a place in life where your dreams felt bigger than your resources? You may have a desire to be who you are dreaming of, but it seems as if the world is against you and your mind is the dictator.

Everyone has the struggle of overcoming the voices around them, and sometimes their own voices, to move to the next level. "Should have," "could have," and "would have" are words manufactured in the factory of excuses disguised as reasons. If we are not careful and intentional, we will permit ourselves to stay seated, waving as our destiny and purpose pass by us. Like a bag of open chips that wasn't consumed in its time, we will become stale and discard ourselves because we think we missed our time and opportunity. Life is hard, and there is no question about that, but we are all living on the byproduct of someone's ability to dream even while everyone and seemingly everything was telling them it was impossible.

"It hasn't been done before" may be the words shot from the barrel of trusted and unsolicited tongues alike whose crosshairs were aimed at your dreams. What would have happened if Dr. Martin Luther King Jr. chose not to dream in a time of immense civil unrest? Some may have thought that it would be impossible to make steps towards equality in a dark time in the USA. What would travel look like today if the Wright Brothers listened to people around them as they snickered at their efforts trying to fly when no one else had done it before? What others saw as science fiction was actual history in the making. Air travel has become such a regular occurrence in our time that when one states that they are going from New York City to Orlando in a few hours, no one thinks twice. Why is that? Because the efforts of those dreamers made a bridge from what had never happened to what is happening. They dared to dream past the step of disapproval of naysayers and haters. They took the used bicycles, crafted an airplane and finally saw what was within them manifest in front of them.

There are countless stories of men and women around the world who took the same journey to see what started as a theory or a thought be transformed into a standard. The unbeaten path that they traveled, which took them from "I wish I could" to "look what I have done" is the same road that you and I must travel. The road isn't paved with smoothed asphalt, lined with polished guard rails, and well-lit by road lights. But in fact, it is a rugged, pitch-black, overgrown toll road that has an immense cost to travel, yet has many exits to leave. That road is called difficulty, and the reason why it isn't traveled upon is that it demands abundant and inordinate effort. Unfortunately, to keep us from traversing on that winding road in the wilderness, we can mentally build a sign held together with nails of fear and anxiety, calling it an impossibility.

Difficult and Impossible

The words "difficult" and "impossible" are words that are used interchangeably in our everyday conversations, but they are vastly different. I firmly believe that if we don't grasp the importance of knowing the difference, then we will continue to tell ourselves that it is okay to be daydreamers instead of day-doers. A simple definition is that "impossible" means that it simply cannot be done. But the meaning of "difficult" is that it can be done but requires immense effort. Unfortunately, we will tell ourselves that the task is impossible and can't be done when in fact it can be achieved but will require considerable effort and will be difficult. Just like animals, we will become ensnared by our laziness and patterns of behavior, telling ourselves, "That is how we always did it."

In nature, animals will travel the path of least resistance. There is a beaten path around rocks and obstacles that is traversed every day to get to water or food. The animal has the ability to crawl or jump over the large rock but will choose to walk around it. This may not seem like a big deal, but the hunters will look on the same path. They are aware that the best place to lay the trap is the spot with the most traffic. Similar to our lives, the road with the most traffic is the highway called laziness, a way of least resistance. The hunter won't place the snare on top of the rock but around it, so that the unaware prey will be caught just while going through life in its typical routine. What have you been telling yourself is impossible, when it only requires effort from you to achieve it? Have you said to yourself that you want to go to college or back to college, yet you continue to talk yourself out of it? "I can't go back to college. We can't afford it." However, you can afford going out to eat every day or picking up the latest pair of stylish sneakers that drop every few weeks. Maybe you can start with one online course rather than a full-time college load.

I hope as you are reading these pages that you have an honest conversation with yourself, because maybe you have been the one benching your dreams while sitting on the sidelines, keeping regret company. We will blame the devil, people, and upbringing way before we take an in-depth look into ourselves and ask, "Am I the one responsible?"

Take inventory of your life as you read these pages. How many things have you started and actually finished? Why did you quit in the process? What have you been telling everyone you are going to do one day, but you haven't even started yet? Have you allowed let down and disappointment to masquerade itself as an impossibility, so you don't have to, again, face the hurt of failure and letdown? This inward excursion through all the excuses may be shocking, especially when you discover that the greatest hindrance to your purpose is perhaps yourself.

I'll start on Monday

Weight loss and fat loss are struggles that many people have around the world. Every New Year, getting in shape is one of the top goals on the list of aspiring individuals. Countless research is done on the latest diet or fad diet to lose the most amount of weight in the least amount of time. Do you do Keto and eat high fats, moderate proteins, and zero carbohydrates? Or maybe you learn to count your macronutrients instead of counting your calories. Do you turn Vegan or go to the polar opposite and jump on the Carnivore diet and only eat meat? After you plan your attack, you head to the nearest sports store and purchase exercise clothing that will wick the sweat as you are inspired to train hard and consistently. But you need the correct shoes, and you want to start doing more compound lifting, so you buy a pair of shoes with a raised heel and also flat sole shoes to be safe.

After binge-watching workout videos on YouTube, you go on your social media and lay out your latest gym clothes in an aesthetic fashion with the best filter and edit. But you can't post it yet until you discover a unique phrase to attach to the picture to make it perfect. After you spent all the money getting the gear, the time researching the diet, and took thirty selfies to find the perfect one, then you make a date for when you are going to start working out. The universal day of the week that is both spoken and unspoken as to when to start anything seems to be Monday. Maybe this sounds like you, but the first week you started on Monday with great anticipation, and for the next few days you were right on track. Then all of a sudden, something happens like a birthday party at work and you binge eat cake, and that derails your plans, and you fall off the disciplines that you created for yourself. But instead of just going back to the charted path to your weight loss goals, the next meal or even the following day, we tell ourselves, "I will start again on Monday." Days pass with you back in your old habits of bad eating and not going to the gym, before you know it Monday passes by again, but this time you don't have the same energy and drive that you had before you started the first time, thus telling yourself that you can't start this Monday. You create an excuse but put makeup on it to look like a reason. This back and forth will go on and on, next thing you know, it is already the following year.

If we wait until Monday to get started on anything, that means we are only giving ourselves fifty-two chances to make the change. Fifty-two opportunities to begin the process to live out our dreams, break an addiction, start the project, and achieve our goals, when in fact, we have 365 days to make the same effort. Have you become an "I'll wait until Monday" kind of person, who is continuing to approve your indifference and procrastination? The time to start is now! The moment to dream is now! Every single second that passes by that you aren't making the steps or effort towards your aspirations are moments in history that you can't get back. Refuse to lie to yourself a moment longer, as if you can't start or continue any day of the week or any other

> Your moment and chance to make a change are on the other side of you, making up your mind to change.

time than Monday. Your moment and chance to make a change are on the other side of you, making up your mind to change.

Powerful or Powerless

Throughout scripture, we can read stories about God using everyday people to do amazing things. But the journey to the *assumed impossible* was crammed full of difficult seasons and moments. Yet, God doesn't take into account things that haven't happened yet or have never been done, because that is far from His equation to formulate the outcome. In fact, when the God of the impossible calls you to do the impossible, He makes the impossible, possible. A most quoted verse that is directly connected to our ability to perform and His mission to empower is found in Philippians 4:13, "I can do all this through him who gives me strength." Here, God has given us a reminder and words of encouragement that we must truly take to heart. We can do all things through Christ. Why? Because we have access to strength and an empowering relationship that comes from Jesus. Christians and nonbelievers alike have quoted or at least heard this verse before, but why are we not living out the statement and promise of the word of God? Why are the areas that God views as attainable in His strength what we view as impossible? May we learn how to see ourselves and our situations in the same way that Jesus does. We are not powerless but powerful. You can write that book; you can overcome depression, and you can start your business. Yet, even with this truth written out for us in the Word of God, do we really believe it? Why do we believe our report before we believe the report of the Lord? Could it be because we don't have faith, but we have a theory?

Faith or Theory

Faith is more than just a theory. A theory is an assumption that is connected to one's own research, experience, or a collected mindset. A theory is an idea of "this could happen" or "this may be the reason." A theory requires a hypothesis and quantifiable degrees of measurement to discover a fact or reveal a truth. I am not knocking the pursuit of knowledge or even science, but it is imperative that we don't place faith in the same pool as theory. A theory is connected to humankind's ability to find out, whereas faith is connected to God's divine faithfulness. With this in mind, when God says that we can do all things through Christ who strengthens us, why do we oftentimes place a "but" at the end of the sentence? Why do we think of God's immeasurable power, yet feel that our situation is too difficult? Do you have a theory that maybe God meant it for someone else but not for you? It is time you take those old dreams that were placed on your bookshelf of forgotten and broken desires, blow off the dust, and start working towards them again. Feed your faith instead of your fear and try again, hope again, and be willing to work again.

In my book, *Crowns are Greater Than Trophies,* I state in the chapter Crowned with Victory, *"you are not to have faith in your faith, but to have faith in God's faithfulness."* Be aware that fighting for your dreams is an uphill battle. There will be moments where seemingly everything has a desire to steal your attention, drive, and purpose. It is challenging to contend when you want to quit; it is tiring to keep writing when you feel as if your mental and emotional pen is without ink. It is hard to keep dreaming when you believe you are living in a nightmare. It is taxing and troublesome to hope after getting told in another interview that you didn't get the job. As is, giving all that you could into a relationship only to have your heart broken again. Standing at the altar in holy matrimony, sharing life-long vows with your husband or wife that yall would be together forever, only to discover later in life that the two of yall would come to an end when someone invited a third and destroyed the covenant on which the relationship was built.

Now you walk through life with sunglasses of hurt and broken-ness, being told to trust again. As grueling as all these moments in life are, the hardest thing to do is to stand back up after you have been repeatedly knocked down. Standing back up and standing all together is a fight in and of itself. But theory or assumption will tell you why to not try again, because the end result will always end in pain, hurt, and failure, whereas faith will proclaim to you to stand back up and keep trying because your breakthrough is closer than you think.

Ephesians 6:10-13-14
[10] Finally, be strong in the Lord and in his mighty power. [11] Put on the full armor of God, so that you can take your stand against the devil's schemes. [12] For our struggle is not against flesh and blood, but against the rulers, against the authorities, against the powers of this dark world and against the spiritual forces of evil in the heavenly realms. [13] Therefore put on the full armor of God, so that when the day of evil comes, you may be able to stand your ground, and after you have done everything, to stand. [14] Stand firm then..."

"After you have done everything, to stand, stand firm." That may sound insensitive to the dynamics and details of your situation, yet it's not the charge to throw in the towel but the command to cultivate an unrelenting gall to continue the fight, which can very well be standing in and of itself. I currently live in Florida, and as I am writing this book, we are in hurricane season. When the hurricanes roll through the state in a slow yet powerful manner, you can see palm trees get so hammered from the 150 mph winds that they bend over and touch the ground. They survived the gust of the storms because they are able to bend and not break, and because the depth of their roots allows them to stand while everything around them seems to fly away.

I believe the roots you need to grow deep in your life are the roots of faith that are connected to God's faithfulness. Tree roots can reach so deep that they will wrap around rocks under the earth. The roots of a tree are like the anchors of a ship that keep it stable in restless and choppy waters. As you continue to read in Ephesians chapter 6, Paul tells the church of Ephesus about the armor of God. The breastplate of righteousness, belt of truth, helmet of salvation, sword of the Spirit, feet fitted with the readiness that comes from the gospel of peace, and lastly, the shield of faith. Every day, we should be ready and equipped with the armor of God, as life is a battle. But may we not forget the shield of faith that is both a defensive and offensive weapon.

Ephesians 6:16
16 In addition to all this, take up the shield of faith, with which you can extinguish all the flaming arrows of the evil one.

This is an essential piece in the armor of God, as it ensures a place of refuge and protection in the midst of the fight. But the material that the shield is created out of isn't forged with ores of our own faith, but of our faith in God's faithfulness. What point would it be in times of battle to exalt our own faith, strength, and abilities? It is excellent to be self-motivators and to encourage ourselves, but that is not what is being elevated. The shield that is being raised, which will smother the fiery arrows of the enemy, has been battle-tested and proven time and time again. When we place our faith in the faithfulness of God and His Word, we have access to a power greater than our own ability and inability to perform. It is a reminder that He is all-powerful, all-knowing, and is contending for you. A powerful passage of scripture that you should memorize is Psalm 91.

Psalm 91:3-6
³ Surely, he will save you from the fowler's snare and from the deadly pestilence. ⁴ He will cover you with his feathers, and under his wings you will find refuge; his faithfulness will be your shield and rampart. ⁵ You will not fear the terror of night, nor the arrow that flies by day, ⁶ nor the pestilence that stalks in the darkness, nor the plague that destroys at midday.

"His faithfulness will be your shield and rampart"! Why is this important to grasp? Because the same God who was with David as he fought Goliath is still alive today. The same God who was with Esther in her season of hardship is fighting by your side. The same Savior who closed the mouths of the lions when Daniel was in the den is still powerful today. The same God who coached Moses through the ups and downs of his life and past his own insecurities to become an instrument of deliverance that God used to free the Israelites from slavery is still raising up voices like him today. The same God who was with Joseph through all of his adversities is still giving promotions today. The same God who healed bodies, delivered the bound, and restored the broken is still doing it all today. We must stop reading the Word of God like a history book or a fairytale because He is still doing the impossible. Not only is He still doing the seemingly impossible, but He desires to do them both in you and through you.

As you dig deeper into this book and your mind and fears start to coach you on all the reasons why these words aren't for you, dig your heels in the ground, and remind yourself of God's promises and the testimonies that you have already experienced. Refuse to press the snooze button of your dream's goals and destiny another time. Get up and wipe the sleep from the corners of your eyes, because "Rise and Shine, it is time to Grind."

CHAPTER 3
WHAT'S IN YOUR HOUSE?

One of the toughest things to do in life is to start. Making the mental shift from "I'll do it one day" to "Now is the time" can be an uphill battle in a torrent of rain. Every time you want to take the step forward to make the climb, you lose your traction and will-power to keep going. Oftentimes, we will tell ourselves that it isn't the right time to start and manipulate ourselves into the belief that later is better than now. Yet it continues a cycle of behavior because tomorrow will become our "later" yesterday very soon. The phrase "one day" can be a cushion we use to authorize ourselves not to live the inceptions of our dreams, as it creates a comfortable pillow for excuses to lay its procrastinating head. "One day" will look for the best time to show up and when all the ducks are in a row. Yet oftentimes in life, the moments to start are rarely convenient but must be seized. Have you been addicted to the drug of "one day"? Do you wake up in the mornings and start the day drinking two "one day" pills and chase it down with coping, to make the excuses easier to swallow? I am by no means attempting to be insensitive to the dynamics of your

> The phrase "one day" can be a cushion we use to authorize ourselves not to live the inceptions of our dreams, as it creates a comfortable pillow for excuses to lay its procrastinating head.

situation, but it is vital that we become honest about what we can change and cannot change. Laziness is best friends with fear, and they will always invite apathy to hang out.

Start Starting

When you open the door of your car and sit in your seat, the next step and the obvious course of action to take is to start the car. If you are expecting to get on the road and head to your destination, putting the key in the ignition or pressing the start button is paramount. If you don't start the car, then you will just be sitting in your mode of transportation, thinking about where you want to go, yet never arriving. It is a frustrating place to be when you are not in motion yet sitting in a place of potential. You can put your seat belt on, adjust the mirrors and tilt the steering wheel to the level and distance of your comfort, yet that still doesn't bring you to your destination until you start the car. You can buy the best all-terrain tires, polish your rims and wash and wax the exterior of the car, yet that will not bring you to your envisioned goal. You will just look good on the outside but remain frustrated on the inside. You can sit in the vehicle and yell at everyone passing you by in the parking lot of possibilities, believing that if you only had their car and life, then you could go, when the harsh reality is that you are still daydreaming rather than "day doing." Start your car!

The best time to start is now, and you can do that even without having everything that you think you need to do it. The first thing that needs to be started is the engine in our minds. If we don't have a made-up mind, then our minds will make something up. A made-up mind is a prevailing weapon that we have access to because it fortifies willpower.

> If we don't have a made-up mind, then our minds will make something up.

Similar to the phrase, "you are what you eat," I believe that you are what you think. Are you living in frustration from the fruits of a made-up mind? Are you in a place of thinking that you are stuck in life and there is no way out and no place to change? Before we ever see a change on the outside, there must be a shifting of thinking on the inside of us.

God is the God of miracles, signs, and wonders. He is the God who hung the stars in the sky as a backdrop for humankind to admire the beauty of His creation. He is the God who placed the planets at the perfect distance away from each other to receive the warmth of the sun, yet not be inflamed by the heat. God is the God who spoke into existence the gravity that keeps us stable on the earth, yet isn't crushing us by its weight and mass. God is powerful, all-knowing, and unstoppable, yet there is one thing that He refuses to do, and that is to mess with our freewill. As much as we would love for the Lord to make up our minds for us, He will not do that. It requires a yielding to say, "God help me," as He pours out His grace upon us to make a choice. But He isn't the one to jump into the driver's seat of your mind, turn the key, and start the engine. We have to make the rational choice to do that. Are we expecting the Holy Spirit to do it for us rather than to empower us to do it? Are we expecting the Holy Spirit to be a smart car that turns, parks, and merges for us, rather than being with us on the journey, dictating the instructions? How many times are we sitting in the comfort of our drivers' seats, bucking and shouting in the altars of our driveways, yet refusing to put our hands on the steering wheel and start the journey? The time is now to start, starting!

Leftovers

Both my mother and my wife are amazing cooks. My wife is from Mexico and makes the best Mexican food that you will ever have. She makes everything from scratch, and the process is time-consuming. Growing up, my idea of Mexican food was a hard taco shell with ground beef, salsa, lettuce, and cheese. If I could go back in time, I would slap that taco out of my hand because it's not an authentic Mexican taco and I have been missing out on a delicious taste bud explosion. A real Mexican taco is a soft corn tortilla with onions, cilantro, homemade salsa and a selection of meat. A few types of meats are carne asada, al pastor, chorizo, lengua, barbacoa, and my personal favorite, tripa or tripe.

The first time my wife and her family wanted to make tamales, I was unaware and ignorant of the extensive and time-consuming process. The family would gather together with massive pots, and the entire kitchen would look like an assembly line. One person would be in charge of preparing the meat, another would prep the corn husk, yet another would prepare the masa. I attempted to help and roll up a tamale, but packed it with too much meat and was kicked out of the kitchen. What seemed like hours and hundreds of tamales later, we were ready and prepared for the holiday season. I noticed how there was extra meat that they didn't use for the tamales and was curious to see what they were going to do with it. After storing it for the next time, a member of the family took it out of the refrigerator and made tacos, which were delicious. After everyone had their fill of tacos and the next meal came around, instead of tacos, this time they made tostadas. Tostadas are a hard, round tortilla with meat, sauce, cheese, and other toppings. The moral of this food journey is that I noticed that nothing went to waste. Everything, no matter how obscure, was used, and it was amazing.

It is essential to know as you are gearing up to fight towards your dreams that God will oftentimes use what you have left. He will use what you have in front of you now and not what you think you need later. The dichotomy is a statement such as, "This is the belief that we are continually looking forward to obtaining a thing/

funds/relationship/position to get started on our journey." But the truth is that just like how the Wright brothers used bicycle parts to craft a makeshift airplane, or Steve Jobs started his business called Apple in his parents' garage, we can commence with what we have in front of us, and more importantly what is within us.

What's in your house?

2 Kings 4:1-7
"The wife of a man from the company of the prophets cried out to Elisha, "Your servant my husband is dead, and you know that he revered the Lord. But now his creditor is coming to take my two boys as his slaves." [2] Elisha replied to her, "How can I help you? Tell me, what do you have in your house?" "Your servant has nothing there at all," she said, "except a small jar of olive oil." [3] Elisha said, "Go around and ask all your neighbors for empty jars. Don't ask for just a few. [4] Then go inside and shut the door behind you and your sons. Pour oil into all the jars, and as each is filled, put it to one side." [5] She left him and shut the door behind her and her sons. They brought the jars to her and she kept pouring. [6] When all the jars were full, she said to her son, "Bring me another one." But he replied, "There is not a jar left." Then the oil stopped flowing. [7] She went and told the man of God, and he said, "Go, sell the oil and pay your debts. You and your sons can live on what is left."

To say that this woman was in a hard place in her life would be a complete understatement. Her husband was dead, and she was living life as a widow in a day and time in history that didn't remotely have the support systems that we lean towards today. Back then, a woman's income, wellbeing, and livelihood were found under the covering of her husband. So when she became a widow, it didn't only affect her emotional wellbeing, but was taking an enormous toll on her and her children's lives. To add more fuel to the fire, people were coming for her two boys to take them away as slaves to work off the debt or loan accumulated from her dead husband. Elisha was a mighty man of God who walked in the supernatural. God used him to perform many signs and wonders, and his reputation preceded him. Her deceased husband revered the Lord and was aware of what God could do.

The way this miracle of provision happened in this woman's life is remarkable, as it was more than just Elisha saying a prayer, but rather giving instructions. It is essential to pause and take notes that at this moment, she could have given up hope and ignored what Elisha was about to ask her to do. On the other side of the desert of risk is an ocean of provision. Elisha asked her, "What do you have in your house?" a question that may come across as extremely irrelevant. Can you imagine the thought the woman may have had in her mind when he asked her such a thing? It is like going to the doctor's office, knowing that you are sick and in need of surgery, and the first question you are asked is what kind of medication you have in your cabinet. Maybe she gave a quick look around to see what she had that would make sense even to meet the overwhelming need. Like the scene in movies of a high-stake poker game, and the one losing his shirt is all out of money, yet in a desperate and stupid act, takes off his wedding ring and places it on the table.

> **On the other side of the desert of risk is an ocean of provision.**

But this woman didn't have anything around her to use as collateral. I grew up in poverty, and I can remember like it was yesterday that when we were broke and in desperate need of the money to buy my brother's medication, the first things to go to the pawn-shop were the items my father assumed had value.

But the man of God was about to use a resource the woman didn't even know was an option to bring her out of the closing walls of despair that she and her family were trapped in the middle of. Like an Indiana Jones movie, a boulder was rolling towards her and her family in narrowing passageways, and the situation seemed hopeless. She told Elisha, "Your servant has nothing there at all." Once again, a factual statement in her situation, when we mentally and mathematically attempt to conjure up an idea to thrust us out of worry into hope. Nonetheless, she told him she had nothing at all, "except a small jar of olive oil." What in the world could a small jar of olive oil do for her and her family? Was she going to pour the olive oil on the driveway and hope the creditors coming for her children would slip and fall? Yet, this trace of olive oil sitting in a small jar would be the seed to her harvest. It would be the instrument of her provision and her place to start.

STEPS

Something happens in the lives of people when our obscurity meets God's divinity. It is at this very moment that the lives of her children were hanging in

> Something happens in the lives of people when our obscurity meets God's divinity.

the balance in the crossroads of belief and disbelief. She could have thwarted the whole miracle that was taking place because the instructions and guidance she was about to receive didn't make sense. How many opportunities in your life have you gambled within moments like this? How many breakthroughs have we stopped because we were waiting for God to lay out a path, rather than just trusting Him to lead our steps? Elisha instructed her to go around and ask all her neighbors for empty jars, and to gather as many she could collect. Once again, take the scenic route in the story and ask yourself what could her neighbors have been thinking about while she was asking for the jars. "What does she need with all of these jars, I wonder?" "Or is she about to do crafts or something?" Can you imagine the looks on the neighbors' faces as she was sharing what she was required to do? Did they look at her like she was strange? Did they have an expression of bewilderment, or some excitement to help? Did any of her neighbors refuse to loan her jars and assumed that she was crazy?

Maybe you have been in this place before as a dreamer and entrepreneur. You shared the startup idea, and they thought you were crazy. Maybe some told you to get a real job, or that might never work. Maybe Thomas Edison was told to give up after the many attempts to invent the light bulb, or Michael Jordan, after not making the cut in the basketball team. I believe this woman had to overcome fear, frustration, doubt, and worry, all the while keeping her hope alive while walking through the steps to her provision. What makes trusting difficult in the moments of hardship is looking in the distance, pondering the goal from afar, yet staring directly down at the steps to take, assuming that they are inadequate.

Psalm 37:23-24 King James Version (KJV)
²³ The steps of a good man are ordered by the Lord: and he delighteth in his way. ²⁴ Though he fall, he shall not be utterly cast down: for the Lord upholdeth him with his hand.

I find it very fitting that the scripture states "the steps of a good man are ordered by the Lord." Because a step is one foot in front of the other, it is an intentional act to tell yourself to keep moving, to keep walking, and to continue dreaming. Yes, we can refer to life as a walk of faith, but I believe that it is better expressed as steps of faith. You have to trust in God's instructions at the moment to lead you to where you are destined and called to be. Please don't overlook or forsake the power of an obedient step if you are aspiring to become a doctor. Take a step, and sign up for your first class. If you are preparing to become a millionaire, that step of learning how to budget your hundreds will aid you to properly steward your future millions. The book that is burning inside of you to be written is only written because of words, sentences, and paragraphs. Instead of viewing the end result in a demoralizing and unattainable manner, remind yourself that you will achieve it in steps.

Shut the door

After the widow amassed the jars from her neighborhood, she was told to "go inside and shut the door behind you and your sons." It is remarkable and a life lesson that we all need to learn how to do every now and again. Sometimes as we are in the process of contending for our miracles, breakthrough, education dreams, and goals, we need to shut out all the noise around us. Some people knowingly and unknowingly can be leeches, sucking out your drive and willpower with their own negativity. Yes, we need realists in our lives in certain seasons to keep us balanced, but when the rubber meets the road, we need encouragers or no noise at all. This is not the only occurrence in scripture when a man or woman of God, and even Jesus Himself shut the door on people. Later in the same passage of scripture, Elisha would lay a dead boy in an upper room, shut the door and see a miracle of resurrection performed. At that moment, he didn't need people saying it couldn't be done, or to give up hope; he needed the power of our miracle-working God. Jesus encountered a dead girl that He had in mind to raise from the dead. But before He performed the miracle, He quieted all the noise and kicked out all the naysayers. In those moments of certain death, a miracle was performed, and she woke up from her decaying and cold slumber.

Do you need to shut the door in your own life? Maybe you need to shut the door to past failures and attempts that keep reminding you why you can't do it. Maybe the painful memories are consistently being rehearsed like a play in your mind, counseling you to not even try again because it will end up the same way, in failure. Is the door that you need to shut made from the opinions of other people, giving you toxic relationship advice derived from their own regrets and failures? Some people will "prophe-lie" instead of prophesy into your life. My wife and I were on the way to our honeymoon, and I opened the door for her to get in the car. All of a sudden, we heard an unwelcomed and unsolicited voice of a woman telling my wife to "enjoy it while you can because that will not happen one day." Sometimes you need to shut the door to the information and voices that aren't pushing you towards your goals, but are pulling you down away from them. If hopelessness and regret have a party, they will always invite hate, jealousy, and envy to hang out.

It is important that you know the difference between a voice that is hating and a voice that is correcting. Just because someone is telling you something that you don't want to hear doesn't mean that it isn't information you need to hear. The scalpel of a doctor is going to hurt, but the surgery to remove the tumor is vital to your own wellbeing. Don't confuse correction and rebuke as hating and condemnation. Many times, that great act of love is to confront an issue and not remain silent rather than watch individuals self-harm and implode.

Pour it out

The actions the widow was taking to save her sons from slavery were remarkable. I wish the Bible gave more information and detail, but she was now at a place where her miracle required her to pour out all her oil. Elisha didn't instruct her to pour out an ounce or a sample, but to pour it all out. Remember, what was the greatest hindrance to her miracle? Was it the jars, the neighbors, her kids, or even the men coming for her kids? No, the greatest hindrance to her breakthrough was herself. She had to overcome the notion of not trusting what she saw and stand on what she heard, while anchoring her belief in what she knew. She was very aware of the amount of oil she had in the little jar, but what could that possibly do in the great scheme of things?

"Pour oil into all the jars, and as each is filled, put it to one side." This is a vital part of this passage of scripture, and it is imperative that we catch the remarkable truth of this miracle. Elisha asked her to use what she had. He asked her to start with what she had available to her in her time of need. Here is the question to pause for a moment and ponder: Are you faithful with your oil? The man of God didn't ask her to wait until she could save up enough money to get more oil. He didn't ask her if she would go to school or complete a program first, then she could start dreaming. God didn't deny her miracle because she didn't have all the resources together, but God used her seed.

The act of her pouring out her oil was like planting and watering a seed. When Elisha asked her to gather empty jars, he knew there was going to be a harvest because her oil was a seed. The act of faith that she took while she tilted the jar to see the oil flow out, watered the seed for her miracle. The act of obedience became rays of hope that shone upon the act, and the jar refused to run empty. We can become so quick to give up or not try at all because we disregard and overlook the power of our seed. The little jar of oil was the embryo that met the seed of her faith and gave birth to the provision that not only liberated her children from the risk of slavery but also sustained her family.

All the jars she gathered were full of oil. She had enough oil to sell it with a massive profit margin, as her overhead was only the small jar of oil. She simply couldn't sit on her provision and expect something to happen. She got up and hustled, sold, and used the blessing that God gave her. The blessing she was given was more than just the oil. It was an opportunity in and of itself. She had to seize the moment, get up, and launch her oil business. She didn't just shout about her blessing, but used it. Has God blessed you just to bless you, or did He bless you to use it as seeds for more blessing? When you get an organic fruit untouched by man's convenience to remove the seeds, it will have the ability to reproduce. Are you sitting in your blessing but not seeing it was your moment to start? You prayed for God to give you a car and now that you have it, are you driving to job interviews? You worked hard to afford the new computer, but now that you have it, have you started the eCommerce business you keep telling people you are going to do one day? You met the man or woman of your dreams after your heart was broken in a horrible relationship, but are you treating that person in the same toxic way you treated the last? What are you doing with your seed? What are you doing with your moment? What are you doing with your time? What are you doing with your oil?

Living in a seed

It is a remarkable thought to know that you are living in a seed. More than likely, the house that you are living in was built of brick, stone, and wood. But how did the building and contractors get the wood in the first place? Could it be because someone along the way planted a seed? They broke the dirt, tilled the soil in the beating heat of the sun in the middle of the day. They watered the seed, maybe being aware they might never see the tree grow large and strong in their own lifetime. But someone along the way is going to reap the benefit from the shade it will give, and maybe the refuge it may be used to create. That seed would be used to create a house, but a loving family will make it a home.

When you finally decide to no longer drag your feet and to plant your seed, you will prepare a harvest that will not only benefit you, but generations to come after you. If you finally start that lawn business with the push lawnmower you have in your garage, you will be able to one day give your family a legacy. Maybe the restaurant you want to start begins today as a food truck, but one day your seed will be used to grow a franchise. You have made up in your mind to draw a line in the sand and break the chains of addiction in your family. Now your children's children will not have to live under the umbrella of that oppression, but can flourish without those chains.

What are you waiting to gather first in order to start? Yes, we would all love more capital and funds, but what can you do with what you have right now? My wife and I travel full-time as Evangelists, and we can remember the struggle all too well. Back then, before all the music was streamed and people owned CD players, we would make our own. We had a printer that we got on Black Friday that printed directly on CDs, but only one at a time. She would make the graphics for the DVD covers and labels, and I would edit the messages in a garage band. It was an all-day event to make a few CDs and DVDs to take with us and place on our product table. But we are so thankful for those seeds that God has used to blossom and grow us. What can you really start today that you have been putting off for tomorrow? You very well could be sitting on the start of your own legacy. No more waiting and no more excuses, your time is now. Stand up from the altar that you have rightly been praying at, asking

God to make a way. Look around your life and in your life, because the way out and the way in may have already been deposited inside of you. God didn't leave you alone, and He hasn't overlooked you in your time of need. Yes, it may only be a little bit of oil, a little bit of time and a small number of resources, but it is time to pour it out.

CHAPTER 4
I CAN'T OR I WON'T

It has been a long day at work, and it seems as if everything that could go wrong goes wrong. You have a report due, but the printer doesn't work. You are in college taking your online final exam that is worth half of your grade, when your WiFi simply stops working. The stress of your day seems overwhelming, and all you want to do is go home and relax. Glancing at your watch or phone every few minutes only makes time inch by even slower. Your shoulders feel like aged and weather-beaten stones, hard and stiff from the fatigue of the last few hours. Your eyes are stinging from the hours being in front of your computer screen. Finally, your time of exodus has come, and you have already planned out your escape and your day. You know that the moment you get home, you are going to kick off your shoes, throw down your keys and make the biggest bowl of cereal that you have ever had in your life and binge on your favorite streaming service.

The keys are in the car, and your foot is on the accelerator, zipping past the grandma sitting upright, unhurried by your hasty pace. Finally, your comfort snack of choice is only a few miles away. You know exactly where your old, torn yet tried and true sweatpants from your high school days, which seem like a cloud of coziness when you put them on, are located. At last, in the distance, your house, and it seems as if it has been waiting for your arrival. Dress shoes are flung in the air simultaneously as the backpack creates a thud on the hardwood floors. Clanging sounds fill the air as cups and bowls bump each other, creating a symphony from the rush of excitement. There might as well be a rainbow emerging from the pantry, because there sits your favorite brand of cereal.

Like any other person, you make a choice to pour out the cereal into the bowl first before pouring in the milk. You are aware of the unspoken rule in "cereal land" that the only reason to pour cereal into a bowl after the milk is for your second or third helping. Unknown to you, a tragedy has taken place, and the news is about to hit close to home. Grasping the jug, you pour it out, only to find out that you are all out of milk.

The travesty of the moment is overwhelming, yet what do you do? The convenience store is only across the street and won't even take you three minutes to get in and out. They're called convenience stores for a reason, being that it is convenient to get in and out off. But even though you desire the bowl of cereal, you debate internally whether it is worth the trip. All day, you have been looking forward to lying on the couch, smashing a bowl of cereal without a care in the world. Yet, you now stand at a crossroads. Do you make the effort to buy more milk, or do you give up on your plan, put the cereal back in the box, and go without the snack?

While making the choice, you go back through the hard drive of your life, mentally clicking on files to remember who was the last person to use the milk and leave it mostly empty. Whose name do you shout out to call attention to blame? Which person would you now spend more time rebuking and correcting because of the obvious error? Ten minutes pass by as you are upset and confrontational, which would have been plenty of time for you to have gone to and come back from the store with a gallon of milk.

At that moment, you have just encountered the shifty troll sleeping under the bridge of many people's consciousness named laziness. Laziness is seldomly vegging out in the slums of regret alone as blame is standing upright with its crooked finger, pointing out an accused victim.

The disease

This may very well be a silly example without any life and death consequences, but it is a moment in life that most people have experienced in some capacity. It's a tug of war with what I can do, need to do, and yet don't feel like doing. It is a slow-eating acid that burns through the toughest of metals. Laziness is an underlining factory that everyone has to confront within themselves. It is a mindset with rigged scales, always balancing comfort over task. It is always trying to slide into procrastination's "DM," telling her sweet and enticing words like "do it later," or "it's not a big deal." Laziness will put other things first, even before your own wellbeing. Laziness will leave you broke and broken while having the ability to work towards your goals, but being counseled to remain down. Like hypertension, also known as high blood pressure, it is a silent assassin and will strike at the least appropriate time.

High blood pressure is an issue that many people in the world have, but at the same time, many ignore because it isn't always connected to a feeling or sensation. It doesn't have a physical sign on your skin or a lump protruding out of a limb or tissue to demand attention. However, it is an underlining issue that can cause strokes, heart attacks, and much more. Regrettably, it takes a trip to the emergency room to wake us up to medicate the need and make a lifestyle change. Why does it take a crisis to motivate us to make the changes that we know we needed to make all along? Why does it take a spouse packing up her and the kids' belongings to move out before the addicted individual finally decides to go to rehab? Why does it take years of being in a dead-end job and frustrated at the world to ultimately choose to further your education or start the business?

Laziness is a chronic disease that all of us have to contend with. It is the rebar embedded in the foundations of excuses. It is oftentimes the blindfolds over our eyes that cause us to stumble moving forward in life. Laziness sits on the opposing shoulder of "purpose," enticing the hearer to believe that "I can't" really is the reason that forward motion towards the fulfillment of your purpose isn't happening. It syphons the energy needed to propel us from thought to mindset and from goals to reality.

I Wish

Simply "wishing" are goals deficient of effort, it is the hope for something to appear when you were asleep that wasn't stewarded efficiently while you were awake. You can see this everywhere in the social media world. In fitness, on Instagram feeds

Simply "wishing" are goals deficient of effort, it is the hope for something to appear when you were asleep that wasn't stewarded efficiently while you were awake.

people are taking selfies in the gym with chiseled abs and sculpted thighs. Yet, on the post, keyboard warriors are swift to type saying such as "I wish I had their genetics" or "It's just steroids." Little do they know, the model and athlete didn't just wake up with muscles but invested hours in the gym. They prep their meals for the week and with great willpower deny themselves the free cake in the breakroom at work. It's easy to look at someone on their mountaintop, admiring the view while disregarding the painful journey from the valley, climbing the steep terrain of effort to get there.

"I wish I had money like them" and assuming that everyone with wealth was born into it is erroneous thinking. What if they accumulated all the wealth because they chose to invest the money that would have been used to go out to eat for the year into stocks or property? Now they generate passive incomes that position them in the lucrative state of life we are admiring. What if we would give a strong look to our own bank statements and discover where the leaks are, plug them and invest? Then we would no longer just wish, but could eat of the fruit of a strong financial portfolio.

I strongly believe that wishing is the same thing as hoping. Hope already has seed in the ground and is connected to a reasonable level of expectation. It is hoping that it would rain because you planted the seed. Hope is birthed from actions, whereas wishing doesn't require effort. If talk is cheap, then wishing is the broken goods on the clearance rack. Wishing is expecting a harvest without sowing any seed.

Hebrews 11:1
"Now faith is confidence in what we hope for and assurance about what we do not see."

I find it amazing that faith is the evidence of things HOPED for and not the things wished for. Why are faith and hope so closely connected? Because they are connected to the same roots of God's word and faithfulness. Whereas wishing is only connected to admiration and happenstance. Stop wishing and start hoping, but make sure you have seed in the ground.

I Can't

There are things in life that are completely outside of our control. A crisis can hit a household that sends life into disarray, or unexpected situations can shift the dynamics of a person's life. I am not so naïve as to say that everything is our fault and we have some areas of control. You couldn't help it when your parents got divorced or when the business you worked for decided to downsize, thus laying you off. You couldn't help growing up in poverty or even growing up in wealth. We can't control natural disasters, and even the random curve balls life seems to have along the way. There are countless things where, as much as we try, control will slip through our fingers. However, we need to have a face-to-face conversation with ourselves to discover the inward truths sewn into the fabric of our personalities.

Toss a bucket of water on the painted face of your "I can't" and make sure that it isn't her evil sister, "I won't," attempting to take advantage of you. It is paramount to our success in life that we are able to discern the difference. As long as we automatically assume that we aren't capable of achieving the goal, we will endorse our own failures. Like driving the same route to work, we can normalize the choice to not act without giving it much thought. Make sure that we are arriving at the destination of "I can't" and pondering if it is factual.

I won't

I believe that, more often than we think, "I won't" makes more appearances in our thoughts and conversations than needed. It is truly the CPU of our life that is affecting what we see and experience through the monitors of our actions. Hints of this reality are found in everyday life, and can cause you to wonder about the sanity of a person. I personally can't stand when people don't put their carts back in the allotted section in the grocery store. I am sure you have seen this yourself, but how many times have you walked past a cart standing alone in a parking space or a foot away from the car? It is shocking to see the amount of laziness, especially when the cart return is only two spaces away.

Laziness really shows up when people don't believe anyone is looking. What adds fuel to the wildfire of lazy living is that it is not the kids that are too lazy to put the shopping cart back in the space right next to them, but the adults. A two-second act can help save someone else hundreds of dollars of repair because the risk of that rogue cart flying into their car is removed because you did your part. Laziness is only concerned with one person, and it is the host of the virus. Yet, the same parents who leave meat in the toy section of the store because they decide they don't want it anymore also rebuke their children for not putting toys back at home. When confronted about the shameful act of waste or inconsiderateness, we will tell ourselves "It's someone else's job." I am very aware that this isn't a popular topic to discuss, but we can see this disease in many areas of life. "I won't" is a deliberate choice, not an absolute standard outside of our control. Once again, being very honest with yourself, are you addicted to "I won't"? Is the embedded excuse of "I won't" keeping you from walking in your purpose?

Tying God's hands

God can do anything, and He is powerful. Attending church services on a weekly basis is a great habit to have, as it can and should be a place of encounter, encouragement, and transformation. However, we can come into a church, in our rooms, cars, or any place and lift up petitions to God. We should have a consistent prayer life that reaches the ears of Jesus. We know that we have strength, resources, direction, salvation, and many other attributes found in His presence. When we are sick, we know that He is a healer. When we are lost, we can find the way out through His Word and voice. It is amazing to have an active and vibrant relationship with Jesus.

A truth in the scripture that we need to make sure we aren't overlooking is how God didn't always do the task for mankind. He instructed them and gave them steps to take, but He didn't do the work for them. When Esther stood before the king in an act of bravery, she had to make the decision herself to get up. When the woman with the issue of blood reached out and touched the hem of Jesus' garment, she had to take the steps. Of course, the supernatural manifestations of God's healing power was something only God could do and give, but the woman took the journey towards them. When God instructed Joshua and the Israelites to march around the fortress called Jericho, God didn't enter their bodies and marched for them, but called them to an act of obedience. At the end of the life of Samson the Nazirite, he called out to the Lord for strength as he stood between two pillars. The Lord did grant him the strength, but He didn't push for him.

Do you see the trend and pattern? It is a thread all through scripture. God gave the increase, strength, healing, and many other things, but He didn't step into them like a car and drive them as He saw fit. There had to be a yielding of obedience and the choice to act. The unwillingness to act upon what God has instructed us to do is like tying His hands behind His back.

Do you see the point and the ripple effect of the thought process that is eating away at your potential? If we don't give attention to the falsely toxic way of thinking, we will attempt to blame God for the state of our life that was in our control all along. God gave Noah the instructions to build the ark, but did God swing the hammer? No, of course not. What would have happened if Noah heard the instructions about the flood, but stood around in the forest, waiting for an ark to just appear? He and his entire family would have been swept away by the same flood that engulfed the earth. It should be alarming if we can water down our church experience to a religious routine. It is a powerful thing when God's grace comes into contact with our effort.

What is remarkable is how little can add to the equation at times, and God works it out. Sometimes you feel you can get it all and other times it's a sacrifice just to show up. God's math doesn't make sense and doesn't add up like ours here on earth. Yet, for whatever reason, God can use "all I have" and turn it into "all I need."

Rest and Laziness

Proverbs 10:5
"He who gathers crops in summer is a prudent son, but he who sleeps during harvest is a disgraceful son"

A tactic that is keeping your purpose at bay is the idea that laziness and rest are the same thing. They may look the same, but they are far from being the same. We must be creatures of rest in many areas of life. Sleep, vacations, and reprieves are all important habits we all need to have in some capacity. I will be the first one to tell you that I am not always good at resting. In fact, I am horrible at it. But without rest, your life and energy would be sucked out of you. Burnout is a very real issue and has affected the lives of many people in the United States of America, and I believe that it is due to the lack of rest.

After God created everything that we hold dear today, He rested. His thundering voice spoke life into existence. He watched as mass and matter were formed. He gazed at the wonder of His creation as trees shot out of the ground and stood at attention. He spoke the separation between land and water as a volcano erupted, creating islands, and as loose dirt became solid. God is the reason why we have fish in the sea and birds in the air. After preparing such an amazing planet, He then created mankind. He gathered dirt, and as a master potter molded the details of Adam and created man. It was on the seventh day of His creation the Bible says that He rested. Rest is a reprieve and time of recovery after the work is done.

Laziness may look like rest, but it chooses to ignore the work that needs to be done. Sleep is supposed to rejuvenate us, but have you ever slept too long? Have you ever slept yourself to the point of being tired? Rest brings you to the gas station to later continue the trip, whereas laziness just turns off the car. It's okay to put on your favorite show and binge watch all the seasons you missed in your time of rest. But if you are dreaming during the time that you are supposed to be grinding, you are forfeiting your chance. Coming to grips with who we really are and the habits that we have is just half the battle. Here is some advice to keep in the forefront of your mind as you are fighting forward and towards your purpose.

Remember your reason

In my offices, both at home and at work, I have pictures of my family. My wife is the most gorgeous woman in the world. She is the kind of woman you would just stop in your tracks and sing slow jams to. I find myself just staring at her pictures on my phone when I am flying around the world preaching, teaching, and educating. Look, she is so attractive that when people find out she is my wife, some literally ask, "How in the world did that happen? Is she blind?" I know without a doubt that I married way up! My son is amazing, and every single day, I count my blessings, because out of all the men in the world, God blessed me with the honor to be his father. He is very adventurous and loves to make people laugh. At the writing of this book, my son Hezekiah is three years old. He is strong, yet compassionate, and bold, yet makes calculated decisions. In addition to that blessing, he is a very handsome "Blaxican" boy. My family is my ministry, and that remains at the top of my priority list.

There are days in my life that I am exhausted and don't want to get out of bed. There are moments when laziness is trying its best to put a chokehold on my purpose, attempting to force the drive to tap out. But what keeps me going along with my faith is my family and the legacy that I am building.

My dad suffered from three strokes that have completely changed his life and way of life. I remember the first time I saw him after the stroke. I held his grandson in my arms, and at that time, he didn't know who I was. Praise God that I wasn't beating myself up with regret, saying that I wish I would have had conversations with my father while I could. I tried my best to make every moment count when I saw him. I told him often "thank you for breaking alcoholism" off our family. He grew up seeing the effects it has on people and made a personal commitment not to get drunk or to drink in general, as a matter of fact. He had his legacy in mind, and even though he could have been lazy about his mission, he always remembered his reason, which was his kids. My dad Kenneth traveled around the nation, singing in a band, and was in plenty of venues where he could have compromised on his goal, yet stayed true. He didn't become lazy in his mission but stayed true to his mission.

What is your reason for you to continue the fight? What are you keeping in the forefront of your mind that pushes you from "I can't and I won't" to "I will, and I am doing"? What drives you to wake up every day and work as hard and smart as you can, so you can rest as best as you can? Whatever your reason is, never forget it. The disease of laziness doesn't care about your goals, dreams, and desires, it only cares about itself. It can feel like quicksand where the more you struggle, the deeper you sink. But the way to get out of that sinking feeling, as laziness sucks you further into excuses, is to allow your reasons to become the rope you grab on to that you use to pull yourself out. What is your reason? This is your chance!

Know your season

It can be easy for us to give up and become lackadaisical regarding our purpose when we don't understand our seasons. When the fight can last too long, we can desire to quit and say enough is enough. Remember your season and stand on the fact that it won't always be winter, because the sun is rising. As I stated in a previous chapter, I currently live in Florida. In the midst of hurricane season we will get rain and horrible storms that are birthed from this season. The question may be asked: If we have hurricanes why are we still staying in Florida? The answer is simple: It's because of seasons. After the hurricane season is over, Florida is an amazing state with great weather. During the night the stars look as if you can reach out and touch them. During the winter months it is perfect, as it isn't too hot and not too cold. Now I won't lie to you, I try to stay inside as much as possible during the summer, as it is blisteringly hot. If my family only judged the state by the hard season, then we would miss out on the good, right before and after it is done. Maybe you are in a hard season in your life right now. You want to be lazy because you feel like your work isn't going anywhere. Yes, it is a hard and demanding season now, but bunker down and endure the storm. The ark that you tarried over will carry you over the choppy waters attempting to flood your life. When it feels like it is getting too hard to handle, remember God's promise in His word.

Isaiah 59:19 New King James Version (NKJV)
"So shall they fear
The name of the Lord from the west,
And His glory from the rising of the sun;
When the enemy comes in like a flood,
The Spirit of the Lord will lift up a standard against him."

Invite others into your mission

A great and effective way for you to punch laziness in the face is to make others aware of your mission. I am not simply saying to post on social media about what you are going to do, but what you are doing. Bring some trusted people into your life who will hold you accountable and encourage you to keep going. Have people who will hold you to your deadline, so you won't keep pushing it off when it is convenient. Here is a fact of life: We all get tired in some way or another. But if you have honest voices speaking into your life, that can help you when things get tough. Being a lone wolf sounds great in theory and may make a good movie, but in reality, we can accomplish a lot in our lives by simply inviting others to hold us to our words. Laziness looks for tiredness as the door of opportunity to step into your motivation and drive it over the cliffs of failure and regret.

> Laziness looks for tiredness as the door of opportunity to step into your motivation and drive it over the cliffs of failure and regret.

Exodus 17:8-13
"8 The Amalekites came and attacked the Israelites at Rephidim. 9 Moses said to Joshua, "Choose some of our men and go out to fight the Amalekites. Tomorrow I will stand on top of the hill with the staff of God in my hands."
10 So Joshua fought the Amalekites as Moses had ordered, and Moses, Aaron and Hur went to the top of the hill. 11 As long as Moses held up his hands, the Israelites were winning, but whenever he lowered his hands, the Amalekites were winning. 12 When Moses' hands grew tired, they took a stone and put it under him and he sat on it. Aaron and Hur held his hands up—one on one side, one

on the other—so that his hands remained steady till sunset. ¹³ So Joshua overcame the Amalekite army with the sword."

The undertaking that God gave Moses and his company sounded simple enough. The ones who had the most to lose were Joshua and the men fighting in the valley. How easy is it to hold your arms up? After all, it is a task that anyone could do, right? If you lift your arms up right now, it wouldn't be much trouble at all, but the longer they hold them, the harder it is to sustain. Easy is nothing but smoke and mirrors that the magician uses to make purpose disappear and pull procrastination out of his hat. When we feel that something is easy to do at the last minute, we wait until the last second to do it. When we feel that something is easy or simple to do, we are most likely not going to ask for help. If you viewed the journey to your purpose as easy and beat your chest, proclaiming, "I got this," you may be rudely awakened by despair and panic.

But Moses had two friends who were with him and aware of his task, so when he got tired, he was able to find rest in his accountability partners named Aaron and Hur. The scripture doesn't give any indication that Moses himself asked for help or that Aaron and Hur saw that Moses needed help. The bottom line is that Moses completed his assignment because he wasn't alone. His friends set him on a stable place and helped carry his mission. In war movies and in times of battle, you will hear soldiers say that we leave no man behind. Even though they may have been injured in battle or even fallen, they don't leave them but bring them home. Moses was losing the battle; thus, the ripple effect of the struggle was affecting Joshua and his men as they fought. Like fellow soldiers laying wounded warriors across their backs, carrying them when they couldn't carry themselves, Moses' friends supported him. As the saying goes, "many hands make light work," and that is true in many areas pertaining to objectives and ambitions. Find accountability and don't be so prideful that you refuse to ask for its support when life gets hard. Invite others into your mission and kick laziness to the curb.

This is your chance! This is your chance to admit yourself into rehab if laziness has been your addiction and drug of choice. Go cold turkey and confront the withdrawals head-on. Laziness will always beckon you back for one more hit because it doesn't like to smoke alone. But you are a changed person, and you want to be clean. Delete Mr. Lazy from your cell phone and ignore his text messages. You aren't being fooled any more with empty words and unfulfilled promises. Tell that "gold digger" named "Mrs. I won't" that you aren't being manipulated by her lies and mischievous ways. The next time she tries to slide into your 'DM,' block her because you don't have time for games. You can't have one-night stands with "I won't" because you are in a committed relationship with your purpose, calling, dreams and goals. She will try to lure you with enticing words while prostituting procrastination on the corners of uncertainty. Yet, again, you aren't cheating and risking the chance to get procrastination pregnant with the child named failure. This is your chance!

CHAPTER 5
FAITH AND FEAR

—•—

While I was writing this book, I never went a day without inspiration and fuel. I meet so many people who are stuck in a place in life that they wish to get out of. It was not too long ago that I felt that I was running in circles in the same hamster wheel. It is easy to watch a late-night commercial about a miracle pill because we never have to take a deep dive into our own behavior. Like a lazy river, many of us have a desire to flop down on a tube and ride the current of another person's efforts. I know I was in that place at some time in my life where I sought for the quickest route to get the best results. Think about how many products out there guarantee fast results, yet protect themselves by adding "some results may vary." The "some results may vary" depend on the individual taking the product and the effort they put in it. This is far beyond weight loss, but with many things in life. We can chase after something that has a track record of working but forget that it is our own depth and dedication that will determine the outcome. If we are going to see the result we are hoping for, it will require dedication, consistency, and boldness. The wrench that the enemy desires to throw into God's plan for our lives is fear, and frankly, we are the ones holding the door open for him to do it.

Fear

Fear is a dangerous, corrosive acid that eats away willpower and passion. It is an adopted excuse because we view it as an absolute. Fear is always pregnant and gives birth to failure, condemnation, and doubt. Fear completely shifts a person's outlook on a situation and gives the benediction before the sermon is

Fear is a dangerous, corrosive acid that eats away willpower and passion. It is an adopted excuse because we view it as an absolute. Fear is always pregnant and gives birth to failure, condemnation, and doubt.

ever preached. Fear looks inwards then outwardly; it takes a sense of our own abilities and limitations. Fear holds a rally in the middle of our heart and mind, and like a political leader attempts to sway unbelievers into its system of thinking. Fear is oftentimes based off sight and not experience. It can grow from "I heard," and not "I have done." Fear is an unknown theory that is powerful because it is a prison without bars and a chain without any links. Fear is the mother of "I cannot," and nurtures her every waking moment. Fear is the belief of what will happen and not always what has happened.

Be very careful, because fear is on the prowl, roaring and snarling at anything in hopes it will submit and not move forward. I believe if you take time to ask most people why they are not moving towards the goals and desires within them, they have a fear of failure. Fear smiles at the thought of intimidation because it motivates the victim to give themselves self-inflicted wounds. Your dream, vision, ministry, and assignment aren't going to manifest themselves; they require you to pursue them. Like a person with agoraphobia, you will never leave your house to make your dreams come true, but sadly, peek at the possibility of it from the slightly opened blinds in the living room. I am aware that there are medical conditions where people suffer from panic attacks, and my prayers are with you. But there are also individuals who don't have a medical condition but have adopted the symptoms due to fear in and of itself. We can worry ourselves sick and stress out until we are ill, and fear is the 007 agent in the shadows.

Fear is the osteoporosis of the mind. It eats away at the bones, standards, and structure that hope stands upon. It leaves our willpower brittle and weak. If the smallest conflict appears, it demands that the host curl up in a fetal position or show its belly. This kind of fear that is bondage is not a mindset God has endorsed and created. The kind of fear that taints your outlook on life as hell here on Earth, isn't birthed from God's heart. Fear was chopped up in the kitchen of the enemy, while we can easily become his waiters, placing the meal right before our eyes.

2 Timothy 1:7 New King James Version (NKJV)
"For God has not given us a spirit of fear, but of power and of love and of a sound mind."

Take a stand with me and decide that it all stops today. I am going to share with you some information that can completely change your life. What I am going to share may shock you, but if you can grasp this truth, it is going to liberate you from yourself. Read carefully and take notes, as school is in session and this is an exam that you can't afford to fail.

Fear and faith are the exact same thing. Yes, you read that correctly: fear and faith are cut from the same cloth. One God endorses, and the other He disdains.

Faith

Faith and fear both come from the same raw ingredient called belief. Belief is the certainty of an outcome that hasn't happened yet. Both cakes and cupcakes have very similar ingredients, and it is up to the baker

Faith and fear both come from the same raw ingredient called belief. Belief is the certainty of an outcome that hasn't happened yet.

to determine which one to make. Similar to that, belief is the batter, and we as the baker can either create fear or faith pastries. Belief is an outlook that isn't always based upon what people have experienced, but on what they have heard. Both faith and fear are the belief in something that hasn't happened yet. How many times have you caught yourself saying, "it could happen" or "it may happen," and even yet "what if it happens?" in a sentence? Well, guess what? You are speaking from a place of belief. What determines if it is faith or fear is the outlook connected to it. Fear is directly connected to our own ability or inability to perform, whereas faith is connected to God's ability to perform. When we have faith, it isn't solely sitting on our own shoulders to make it happen, but we understand we serve a God who is standing by His word. We keep praying for more faith, when in fact we are operating in it every single day, but we have polluted faith and made it fear. Read the conversation Jesus had with this man regarding his son.

Mark 9:22-25
22 "It has often thrown him into fire or water to kill him. But if you can do anything, take pity on us and help us." 23 "'If you can'?" said Jesus. "Everything is possible for one who believes." 24 Immediately the boy's father exclaimed, "I do believe; help me overcome my unbelief!"

²⁵ When Jesus saw that a crowd was running to the scene, he rebuked the impure spirit. "You deaf and mute spirit," he said, "I command you, come out of him and never enter him again."

Instead of asking for more faith, maybe our prayers and desires should be to ask the Lord to help us with our unbelief. I hope you see how monumental this truth is and how it can truly help you walk and live in victory. The word of God is packed full of promises and inspirations about the works of God. They are written for us to learn from and be inspired by, but also to let us know that the same God who did it before can and will do it again. He is still a Healer, Savior, and Way-Maker, and you must believe that He can do it for you. What if your victory and success are on the other side of your outlook on the situation?

Tourist

In 1 Samuel 17, a young man named David had a life-changing moment in his life that paints the perfect picture of faith and fear. A story that many have heard and quoted since they were young, holds an antidote to poisoned faith. It is important that you don't read past this story because you have heard it before. Pride places a blind-fold on our eyes and earmuffs on our ears and labels its assumptions. Become a tourist in the word of God, embracing every detail and capturing every moment. The story of David and Goliath is filled with pit stops on the way to the climax where a young man finds victory even in the midst of unfeasible odds. As we journey through the passage of scripture, I am going to pull the double-decker bus over and fill you in with much-needed details to understand the gravity of the moment. As mentioned, before we took the highway, to appreciate the destination we must grasp the journey. Hello, my name is Timothy, and I am your tour guide for today.

Champions

1 Samuel 17:1-51
Now the Philistines gathered their forces for war and assembled at
Sokoh in Judah. They pitched camp at Ephes Dammim, between
Sokoh and Azekah. ² Saul and the Israelites assembled and camped
in the Valley of Elah and drew up their battle line to meet the
Philistines. ³ The Philistines occupied one hill and the Israelites
another, with the valley between them.

There was a great battle that was about to take place, and the
grounds from which they fought seem right out of a movie. The
Israelites were standing at attention and ready for battle on one high
hill, and the opponents were on another high hill. The battle was
supposed to take place in the valley between them. Both armies
could see each other from the comfortable positions that were free
from any act of violence. From their current positions, they could
only view the battlefield, but if victory was going to be won they had
to leave the comfortable and safe place to fight what was fighting
them. Even in life, half of the battle seems to be to take the first
steps out of our comfort zone into the war zone. The battlefield that
many can find themselves stuck being so close to, is the war that is
waged within them. The Israelites would soon discover that there
were two battles taking place: the battle before them and the battle
within them.

⁴ A champion named Goliath, who was from Gath, came out of the
Philistine camp. His height was six cubits and a span. ⁵ He had a
bronze helmet on his head and wore a coat of scale armor of bronze
weighing five thousand shekels; ⁶ on his legs he wore bronze greaves,
and a bronze javelin was slung on his back. ⁷ His spear shaft was
like a weaver's rod, and its iron point weighed six hundred shekels.

*His shield bearer went ahead of him. ⁸ Goliath stood and shouted
to the ranks of Israel, "Why do you come out and line up for battle?
Am I not a Philistine, and are you not the servants of Saul? Choose
a man and have him come down to me. ⁹ If he is able to fight
and kill me, we will become your subjects; but if I overcome him
and kill him, you will become our subjects and serve us." ¹⁰ Then
the Philistine said, "This day I defy the armies of Israel! Give me
a man and let us fight each other." ¹¹ On hearing the Philistine's
words, Saul and all the Israelites were dismayed and terrified.*

Comes by hearing

A vital point to see in the Israelites' interaction with Goliath is
that it wasn't only his stature and strength that intimidated them.
I can only imagine them hearing the echo due to the valley from
the baritone voice of the giant taunting them. Goliath was a massive man and was so tall that his head could almost touch the rim
of a ten-foot regulation basketball goal. He was not only big but
also strong, and that added to the overwhelming task to fight him.
However, I don't believe that it was only Goliath's size that made
them so scared, but more so his reputation. The Bible doesn't intro-
duce him as a giant even though the writer does give us the details
of his size. The scripture repeatedly introduces Goliath as a champion. He was someone who wins and repeatedly wins, an overcomer
with a long record of victories. I wonder, if he didn't have the reputation of being victorious, would they have been so scared? What
if he was just big but weak, large yet always lost? But this wasn't the
case. He was a winner, and everyone knew it. As they looked from
afar from the perch of their safe places and comfort zones, they may
have already told themselves that there was no way they could win.

They heard his offensive words challenging everyone to a duel and hearing the consequences, yet no one took the steps down into the valley to face him man to man. They were sick of fear and frozen in doubt. It is imperative that we see they gained the conclusion that the battle couldn't be won solely from what they saw and heard. They believed it was a checkmate in the very battle before them, without even moving a piece. Their fear was being fed from the same gateway where our faith grows, by what we see and hear — terrified by a bully who never shot an arrow or swung a sword, like statues stuck in a place, not from experience but from what-ifs and maybes.

Romans 10:17 New King James Version (NKJV)
"So then faith comes by hearing, and hearing by the word of God."

Faith comes by hearing and hearing by the word of God. We are encouraged and strengthened from the testimonies we read in scripture and have experienced ourselves. Our faith is lifted when we hear about what God did for others and is still doing today. The same road that information travels along has two destinations the driver can choose from: fear or faith. There can be two people in the room who hear the same information, yet believe two outcomes. We must be people who stand on a solid and unmovable position of faith that is rooted and established in the Lord. The scriptures tell us they were dismayed and terrified. Dismayed is an important word to look into, because it gives even more context to the story and dynamics of the battle brewing within the warriors.

Dismayed is the consistent breaking and tearing down of bravery and courage. It wasn't as if they never had the brave intention to fight, but when they heard the onslaught of the disheartening words, a transaction took place. A transfer from faith to fear transpired solely off information and hearing. Have you been to places in your life where you were dismayed? The champions in your life you attempted to attack with high hopes left you low in spirit. You hyped yourself up to finally ask for the raise you told yourself you deserve, only to be shot down. You built up the willpower to launch your business but encountered the hardships of dealing with employees and payroll. Whatever the case may have been, maybe your courage became discouragement through the fear of losing and failure. You started with great intentions, dressed for the occasion and cleared out your schedule for the arrival of "victory," only for him to set you up yet once again, eating alone in the restaurant of expectation. But just like many actions movies, don't lose hope during the plot twist because the end credits aren't rolling yet.

High school fights

12 Now David was the son of an Ephrathite named Jesse, who was from Bethlehem in Judah. Jesse had eight sons, and in Saul's time he was very old. 13 Jesse's three oldest sons had followed Saul to the war: The firstborn was Eliab; the second, Abinadab; and the third, Shammah. 14 David was the youngest. The three oldest followed Saul, 15 but David went back and forth from Saul to tend his father's sheep at Bethlehem. 16 For forty days the Philistine came forward every morning and evening and took his stand. 17 Now Jesse said to his son David, "Take this ephah of roasted grain and these ten loaves of bread for your brothers and hurry to their camp. 18 Take along these ten cheeses to the commander of their unit. See how your brothers are and bring back some assurance from them. 19 They are with Saul and all the men of Israel in the Valley of Elah, fighting against the Philistines."

For forty days, the champion came out, ready to fight and end the battle, and not a person stepped up to the task. A young man named David would have been the last person many would have thought to be the victor of this story. He came from humble beginnings and was faithful to his task to tend to his father's sheep. His dad Jesse wanted an update of the assumed epic battle that was taking place. Like Uber Eats, David had a food order that he needed to deliver to his brothers who were fighting. Jesse wanted news of the battle, but the only thing they were fighting was fear.

> [20] *Early in the morning David left the flock in the care of a shepherd, loaded up and set out, as Jesse had directed. He reached the camp as the army was going out to its battle positions, shouting the war cry.* [21] *Israel and the Philistines were drawing up their lines facing each other.* [22] *David left his things with the keeper of supplies, ran to the battle lines and asked his brothers how they were.* [23] *As he was talking with them, Goliath, the Philistine champion from Gath, stepped out from his lines and shouted his usual defiance, and David heard it.* [24] *Whenever the Israelites saw the man, they all fled from him in great fear.*

David finally arrived at the destination, maybe expecting to see a blood-soaked battlefield crowded with dead bodies and wounded warriors. But their armor was still shiny and the swords still sharp. If there was any conflict in those last forty days, it could have been within the army due to the high emotions and stress, but it wasn't against Goliath. Going through the motions, and at his point the routine, they lined up for battle, shouting the war cry. They got dressed, picked up the weapons, walked out of the tent, and went to the same place and yelled. The war cry was supposed to intimidate the enemy and encourage the individual and other brothers-in-arms. But at this point, still being taken advantage of by fear, they were only yelling and maybe had no intentions of fighting.

I strongly believe that this is the lives of many people; they are shouting about things that they aren't willing to fight for. Just like the Israelites, we can put on our Sunday best, load up the car and head to church. We will worship and hear a powerful and challenging sermon while shouting amen. An altar call is given from the minister, and we will go up and respond, crying to the Lord for His intervention. We shout in victory and give God a sacrifice of praise, but leave the church, go out to eat, but don't fight for the victory on Monday. The word of God is inspiring, uplifting, and challenging, and with God's grace, we can become better every passing day. Are you at the altar of your church every Sunday, shouting for God to heal your finances, but refusing to fight for it by creating a budget? Maybe you are going through health issues that are connected to being overweight or eating unhealthy. If so, have you been praying for God to heal your body, but when it comes to the moment to fight by getting on a diet or going to the gym, are you telling yourself that you can't? The Israelites and the Philistines were having old school high school fights. They figuratively inflated their chests, put their heads together and got into each other's faces. "You talking junk" or "What you say about my momma?" They were doing nothing but exchanging words, not blows. Yet, again the longest bridge to cross over is the abyss of fear that is within our own minds.

Fear of Man

25 Now the Israelites had been saying, "Do you see how this man keeps coming out? He comes out to defy Israel. The king will give great wealth to the man who kills him. He will also give him his daughter in marriage and will exempt his family from taxes in Israel." 26 David asked the men standing near him, "What will be done for the man who kills this Philistine and removes this disgrace from Israel? Who is this uncircumcised Philistine that he should defy the armies of the living God?" 27 They repeated to him what they had been saying and told him, "This is what will be done for the man who kills him." ²⁸ When Eliab, David's oldest brother, heard him speaking with the men, he burned with anger at him and asked, "Why have you come down here? And with whom did you leave those few sheep in the wilderness? I know how conceited you are and how wicked your heart is; you came down only to watch the battle."

²⁹ "Now what have I done?" said David. "Can't I even speak?" ³⁰ He then turned away to someone else and brought up the same matter, and the men answered him as before. ³¹ What David said was overheard and reported to Saul, and Saul sent for him.

Even with all the gifts, status, and even marrying into the royal family, that wasn't enough to cause any of the warriors to fight Goliath. David heard all the benefits of confronting the champion and winning, which was an added reward for his task at the end. David came to the battle with great intentions and under his father's instructions. He had a mission in mind, and just like everyone that lives today, you will always have people who believe in you and others who don't. In this case, his own family and brothers belittled him. Before David ever had to confront Goliath, he had to combat the hateful words of his brother. Eliab attacked him and his character without cause. It was good for David and would benefit all of Israel that he didn't stop in his tracks because people didn't believe in him. He wasn't looking for approval from Eliab, and he didn't need it either.

I wish the scriptures gave more insight into the conversation to know the emotional climate. They had been on the battlefield for over forty days and consistently hearing about Goliath. In times of stress, people are quick to be short-tempered with other people. Like in our lives today, in a state of self-preservation, they may have started to play the blame game. Could they have been tearing each other down with their words, and David happened to walk into the crossfire? I don't believe this theory is farfetched in the slightest, as this kind of thing happens every day. Psychological displacement and transference are such a part of some people's lives that it is a natural as breathing.

For example, you are at work, and the boss is having a bad day. Maybe he or she got a bad report and the profit and loss helped turn their joy into anxiety. Now you get to work without doing anything wrong, and they have a horrible attitude and raise their voice at you. You so badly want to take off the earring and the rings and host an untelevised boxing match between yourself and their face, but you decide not to because you need the job. So you are typing on your computer, smashing the keys harder and harder with every stroke as if they are the source of your stress. Finally, your lunch break arrives, and you don't even care about your diet at the moment and want to stress eat, so you head to the nearest fast food drive-thru.

You order your burger without mayo and onions as you always do, but they add extra mayo and onions and forget the pickle. Now you are infuriated, so you walk to the counter and give the cashier a horrible attitude, telling them how they can't do their job and other colorful words. Snatching the redone order one of the teenagers hands you, you storm through the doors because you have to get back to the office. The hours feel like days, but it is finally time to clock out, and you can't wait to get home. Speeding out of the parking lot, you honk your horn at the car in front of you that is driving the speed limit, but you think they should be in a hurry because you are. At last you're home, and your kids have more energy than a power plant, and your spouse bombards you with tasks and questions before you even get a chance to set your things down. With your last nerve completely tapped out, you yell at your kids for no reason and belittle your spouse.

Now, the family you are at work to provide for, you have just pushed them away and torn them down with your nasty attitude, demeanor, and words. Now the kids who missed you during the day don't even want to be around you. Your spouse who had a date night planned that you forget about doesn't even want to go out now. Why? Because your boss raised his voice at you. These series of events happen every single day. Sadly, the ones who take the beating because we displace and transfer our stress are our families and not the one who caused it. When I read David's conversation with his brother, Eliab, I see a stressed-out person who is displacing and transferring his own stress upon his own family member. David response to Eliab was something that we all need to learn how to do. He didn't let it phase him, he turned around to someone else, and continued in his pursuit.

The fact of life is that not everyone is going to like you and support you. Stop looking and seeking for the approval of people who aren't even connected to your dreams. The only approval David needed at that moment to fight Goliath was King Saul. Maybe you are trying to better yourself, your ways, and break bad habits. Be free from the fear of man, open your wings, and soar to your uncharted territories. Eliab was going to put handcuffs on David and keep him at his level or supposed place. Beware of the people who don't want you to succeed because they aren't succeeding. As the saying goes, "misery loves company," so don't answer the phone when they are calling.

You're a Champion

32 David said to Saul, "Let no one lose heart on account of this Philistine; your servant will go and fight him." 33 Saul replied, "You are not able to go out against this Philistine and fight him; you are only a young man, and he has been a warrior from his youth." 34 But David said to Saul, "Your servant has been keeping his father's sheep. When a lion or a bear came and carried off a

sheep from the flock, [35] I went after it, struck it and rescued the
sheep from its mouth. When it turned on me, I seized it by its hair,
struck it and killed it. [36] Your servant has killed both the lion and
the bear; this uncircumcised Philistine will be like one of them,
because he has defied the armies of the living God. [37] The Lord who
rescued me from the paw of the lion and the paw of the bear will
rescue me from the hand of this Philistine." Saul said to David,
"Go, and the Lord be with you."

Full of faith, drive, and vision, David approached Saul and gave
him the big news that he would fight Goliath. Saul didn't leap with
joy when he heard David's words because to him there wasn't any way
he could win. Once again, another battle was about to take place, a
fight, even more, Goliath was confronted. David had to overcome
the temptation to quit while other people were discounting him.
The raw and a simple fact of life is that on the mountain climb to
success, there will always be stones rolling or thrown in your direction. Saul may not have meant any harm with what he was saying,
but that doesn't mean that it didn't hurt. As hard a pill as it was to
swallow, King Saul was speaking factually. But man's fact may not
always be God's truth. It was a fact that David was young, and it was
a fact that Goliath was bred to be a warrior since his youth. But it
was not factual to believe that David wasn't ready for the fight or
wasn't qualified to confront the champion. Why? Because David
was a champion himself.

The future King David had an ace up his sleeve that would cut
the entire deck of fear and excuses. He also had experiences during
his time as a shepherd that prepared him for this moment in his
life. He had a testimony birthed in crisis that gave him the experience and strength to believe with such confidence that he could
fight. King Saul and the rest of the Israelites were dismayed by the
winning record of Goliath. David wasn't fazed. He didn't inflate

his ego, beat his chest, and stand upon assumptions and pride. His strength flowed from the faithfulness of God, the covenant that He had with him, and the battles He bought him out of. While David was watching his father's sheep, a lion and bear carried off a sheep. Most people would have said, "Well, we just lost a sheep, and there is nothing I can do." David ran after it, grabbed the massive animals, and killed them. The future king conquered the king of the jungle.

The question that comes to mind while reading this story is why King Saul would give David permission to fight. Was it because he was moved by elegant words, or was David an amazing salesman? I believe it was the fact that David's testimony pointed to the strength of God and how God could intervene. All that was required was a brave person who trusted God deeply, and he was right in front of Saul's face. David knew he had power and a covenant with God, and the raw fact was that everyone had the same chance to step into this truth as David did. Everyone could have believed God and taken the step of faith, yet they jumped in fear and stayed there. When Saul gave David his thumbs up to fight the champion, I believe he believed he wasn't placing their lives in the hands of a little boy. But they placed their lives in the hands of God, whom the young boy trusted.

The conversation David had with Saul is powerful and brings truths that we must instill in our lives every day. All throughout this passage, people were scared of a man they never fought but only heard about and saw. Fear filled them to the brim of their thought life, and placed handcuffs on their willpower, as they didn't resist its arrest. But when David heard the same words of Goliath, he was able to filter out fear because of the faith that resided within him. There is a difference between confidence and pride that we have the fortune to see displayed in this powerful passage. Goliath was prideful and stuck on himself, highlighting his strengths and past performances. Whereas David was confident, yet his assurance wasn't in or on himself, but on God. The giant's fear was spread because of what he could do and what he said. When David spoke, faith was sown into the heart of Saul and would soon bring a harvest of victory in which everyone would benefit from.

[38] *Then Saul dressed David in his own tunic. He put a coat of armor on him and a bronze helmet on his head. [39] David fastened on his sword over the tunic and tried walking around, because he was not used to them. "I cannot go in these," he said to Saul, "because I am not used to them." So he took them off. [40] Then he took his staff in his hand, chose five smooth stones from the stream, put them in the pouch of his shepherd's bag and, with his sling in his hand, approached the Philistine. [41] Meanwhile, the Philistine, with his shield bearer in front of him, kept coming closer to David. [42] He looked David over and saw that he was little more than a boy, glowing with health and handsome, and he despised him. [43] He said to David, "Am I a dog, that you come at me with sticks?" And the Philistine cursed David by his gods. [44] "Come here," he said, "and I'll give your flesh to the birds and the wild animals!" [45] David said to the Philistine, "You come against me with sword and spear and javelin, but I come against you in the name of the Lord Almighty, the God of the armies of Israel, whom you have defied. [46] This day the Lord will deliver you into my hands, and I'll strike you down and cut off your head. This very day I will give the carcasses of the Philistine army to the birds and the wild animals, and the whole world will know that there is a God in Israel. [47] All those gathered here will know that it is not by sword or spear that the Lord saves; for the battle is the Lord's, and he will give all of you into our hands." [48] As the Philistine moved closer to attack him, David ran quickly toward the battle line to meet him. [49] Reaching into his bag and taking out a stone, he slung it and struck the Philistine on the forehead. The stone sank into his forehead, and*

he fell facedown on the ground. [50] So David triumphed over the Philistine with a sling and a stone; without a sword in his hand he struck down the Philistine and killed him. [51] David ran and stood over him. He took hold of the Philistine's sword and drew it from the sheath. After he killed him, he cut off his head with the sword. When the Philistines saw that their hero was dead, they turned and ran.

An overlooked, cast aside, belittled young man with purpose, willpower, and destiny found victory over seemingly impossible odds. Can you imagine the expressions of the armies when David first walked down into the valley to fight? Remember, the pact was made that whoever would lose would be the slaves and subjects to the other. The whispers and perhaps yells in the crowd as they saw the hands in which Saul placed all their lives in. Not a strong man hurling boulders like soda cans or a powerlifter bench pressing a car, but a boy who could pass as their sons. If they had cell phones back then, maybe they would have updated their social media platforms with mean status and final goodbyes. *How could Saul agree to this? This is our end?* For over forty days and at least eighty times, they had heard their fears yell at them from a distance and become the professor in their minds. David would soon prove them wrong because at no point in this entire story did he believe he could do this alone. He knew his strength and drive came from the Lord.

Yet again, David's youth was brought to his attention as if his age disqualified him. First Eliab, then Saul, and now Goliath poked fun at him. The champion was putting his attention on the young boy's stature and weapons of choice. David talked right back, highlighting that God fought on his side. David charged toward the nation's fear in the flesh with courage and laser focus, spinning the sling and hurling a stone toward the forehead of the giant. It sank into his skull like a foot walking through wet sand. Like forest workers yelling "timber!" the champion went down, suffering his only and yet fatal loss.

Defeating my champions

The story of David and Goliath is remarkable, and much deeper than the superficial way we can hear it explained. It's more than just a young boy defeating a giant, but the victories that happened along the way. It is a dynamic passage where the effects of fear and faith can be clearly seen. What are the champions in your life that you have been telling yourself you can't defeat? What has been hounding you every waking day, pointing fingers at your inability to overcome the obstacle? What have you been avoiding and pushing off because you don't want to confront it? Procrastination can hide the fear in plain sight because it is our permissible way to avoid the issue. What have you been yelling at in the distance, posting about on your social media about how you would confront it, but never do? Is furthering your education standing across from you, telling you that you are too stupid? Is the fear of failure wagging its finger in your face, telling you that it is better not to act because at least it is safe? What have you been afraid of?

> Procrastination can hide the fear in plain sight because it is our permissible way to avoid the issue.

As you have seen in the last few pages, you have been more than just afraid. You have been having faith that things will end badly. You have been having faith that you will get rejected if you ask for the raise. Maybe you have been having faith that because everyone else in your family hasn't started a business, then it can't be done. Whatever the excuse that has been yelling at you for all this time, maybe it's time to redirect your faith. The issue has never been you not having enough faith, as in measurements and volume. You have an abundance in which you have been drowning. The issue is that your faith has been tainted with inadequacies, low self-esteem, and bad reports. Your faith has been hijacked by your own efforts and self-righteousness. The blood of your belief has become toxic, and it is time for your dialysis appointment.

It's time to cleanse your life-giving blood of impurities and readjust your belief systems. The reality check is that your dirty faith may have placed you in the situation you are in right now. You saw yourself as not making it, struggling and alone. You kept telling yourself that you can't do it and you tried before? Behold, you are living out your faith. Fear and faith come from the same womb, but raised by different parents. Turn your fear into faith and conquer your champions. Step out of your safe place, padded with excuses and wishes. Pick up your sling and run toward that giant, conscious of the fact that you aren't fighting alone. This is your chance!

CHAPTER 6
WHAT'S IN YOUR HANDS?

———•———

Everyone walking the earth today, and in the past, has experienced insecurities in some form or another. It seems as if the whisper within you is always louder than the voices of encouragement around you. Trusted individuals can proclaim on the mountaintops about your greatness and ability to perform, yet at the same time, you just have a difficult time seeing yourself the way they see you. Our own insecurities will always be the cords of uncertainty that we can be entangled in. It is a thought life, void of an internal fortitude to complete the task or even be qualified to start. Insecurities are the infamous inward voice that leaves us motionless, viewing our potential on the horizon. As long as we keep listening to that voice that speaks from a soapbox of assumptions, we will never walk into our purpose. God is yelling, "You can do this," and we are yelling back, "No, we can't."

Insecurity is simply not secure in anything. It is the emotional drive that longs for more before it can even think about starting. It will play a dangerous comparison game with everyone else, longing to have what they have, all the while disregarding what you possess. It is an unstable minion having a temper tantrum in our mind, waiting to have it his way. It flees challenges and grows in an incubator created with comfortableness such as "one day" and "I'm not able." As a constant and nonstop drip on a faucet, it is an annoyance at its best. We all have to fight it and make sure that insecurities are not leading us away from our desires and purpose.

When we read in scripture, we can find many stories where God used men and women who battled insecurities and anxiety. When God called them into their purpose, it wasn't as if He was surprised about the mental struggles they had. He used them because and even in spite of, yet He walked with them to overcome them. We serve a God who isn't interested in our excuses of why we can't start and take the chance, especially if He is calling and equipping us to take the leap. I believe God will father us and help us to walk through life to learn and trust along the way. There isn't a single example in the word of God where God commissioned a man or woman to be used that He accepted their insecurities, concerns and fears as legitimate reasons why they couldn't start being used.

I am very aware there are real needs and requirements to do anything in life. If you want to have a business, you need equipment and maybe capital. If you go to college, you will need scholarships and aid to get there. There are very practical needs to sustain a business and dream that can't be taken away. However, we can be so overwhelmed by the needs of the future that we take zero steps towards our goals in our present. You may need thousands of dollars for the latest lawn equipment to sustain your lawn company, but can you start with a push mower that you already own? You may need a storefront in the growing part of town to have your barbershop, but can you start in your home to build your clientele? This is your chance, and the time to step is now! You may be surprised, but God can use what is in your hands. Just ask Moses.

Moses' life seems like an intense movie of suspense, drama, action, and science fiction moments. He witnessed signs and wonders on a regular basis and was used to be the instrument to deliver all of Israel out of Egyptian slavery. It would be a mistake to just read in the middle and the end of his life journey and endeavors, and thus believe that he was always brave and bold, when in fact, he was fearful and felt completely unqualified. However, with everything in life, God desires to walk with us and brings us to an awareness of His grace and power. Your life can shift right now by understanding this simple truth: it is not possessions that grant us power, it is position.

The Calling

During the time that God was raising up Moses, the Israelites had been living as slaves. They had been in bondage for over 430 years, feeling the weights of chains and the cracking of whips. Generations to generations, fathers, grandfathers, and great-grandfathers were in bondage until God commissioned a man to make a difference! Not a perfect man, and at first not even a willing man. There were generations who were born and died while in slavery, never knowing what a free life felt like. Never knowing what life was like outside of a master demanding things to be built, work to be done, that they would never lift a finger to do themselves. Generations under the bondage of slavery, never knowing what it would be like to worship in freedom and live in peace. But God heard that cry and raised up a man named Moses who was in slavery himself. But the slavery he was going through wasn't like the other Hebrews. The bondage he was fighting wasn't iron chains around his ankle but the chains around his mind, spirit, and emotions. His master didn't carry a whip but used words to keep his subject in line and control. He didn't have to threaten him with violence, but just used worry and anxiety. Moses was a slave to his own insecurities and fears, but God became his deliverer. God wrote out the Emancipation Proclamation for Moses' internal battle and held his freedom papers in His hands.

Exodus 3:1-15

"Now Moses was tending the flock of Jethro his father-in-law, the priest of Midian, and he led the flock to the far side of the wilderness and came to Horeb, the mountain of God. ² There the angel of the Lord appeared to him in flames of fire from within a bush. Moses saw that though the bush was on fire it did not burn up. ³ So Moses thought, "I will go over and see this strange sight—why the bush does not burn up." ⁴ When the Lord saw that he had gone over to look, God called to him from within the bush, "Moses! Moses!" And Moses said, "Here I am."

⁵ "Do not come any closer," God said. "Take off your sandals, for the place where you are standing is holy ground." ⁶ Then he said, "I am the God of your father, the God of Abraham, the God of Isaac and the God of Jacob." At this, Moses hid his face, because he was afraid to look at God. ⁷ The Lord said, "I have indeed seen the misery of my people in Egypt. I have heard them crying out because of their slave drivers, and I am concerned about their suffering. ⁸ So I have come down to rescue them from the hand of the Egyptians and to bring them up out of that land into a good and spacious land, a land flowing with milk and honey—the home of the Canaanites, Hittites, Amorites, Perizzites, Hivites and Jebusites. ⁹ And now the cry of the Israelites has reached me, and I have seen the way the Egyptians are oppressing them. ¹⁰ So now, go. I am sending you to Pharaoh to bring my people the Israelites out of Egypt." ¹¹ But Moses said to God, "Who am I that I should go to Pharaoh and bring the Israelites out of Egypt?" ¹² And God said, "I will be with you. And this will be the sign to you that it is I who have sent you: When you have brought the people out of Egypt, you will worship God on this mountain." ¹³ Moses said to God, "Suppose I go to the Israelites and say to them, 'The God of your fathers has sent me to you,' and they ask me, 'What is his name?' Then what shall I tell them?" ¹⁴ God said to Moses, "I am who I am. This is what you are

*to say to the Israelites: 'I am has sent me to you.'" ¹⁵ God also said to
Moses, "Say to the Israelites, 'The Lord, the God of your fathers—
the God of Abraham, the God of Isaac and the God of Jacob—has
sent me to you.' "This is my name forever, the name you shall call
me from generation to generation."*

I am who I am

Our own uncertainties and timidity will become the very stum-
bling blocks used to trip us and keep us down. Keep in mind that
this story isn't a fairytale and hasn't been enhanced with a figure
of speech. Moses encountered God in a supernatural manner and
was still having a hard time putting his head around the fact that
God was calling him. He experienced a tug of war with what he was
seeing and hearing against what he believed and knew. The bush was
on fire and not burning, and to add to the amazement, the God of
the universe was talking to him and knew his name. It should bring
us a great level of confidence that we can do the things that God has
called us to for the simple fact that he is calling us. But once again,
Moses' fear and doubt is attempting to take advantage of him.

God was calling him back to the very place he ran from. After
the murder that he committed, and running away from the people
he grew up with, he didn't want to go back. I find it amazing how
God will oftentimes anoint and appoint us to help other people
out of the muck and mire that we used to be stuck in. Moses could
no longer run from his past but face it head-on. His cup of stress
was about to run over and overflow into the anxiety he was already
swimming in. Recall Moses first words to God after telling him to
go back to Egypt and free his people: "Who am I that I should go to
Pharaoh and bring the Israelites out of Egypt?" He asked, "Who am
I?" a question that insecurities keep repeatedly asking in our daily
lives. Who am I to go and ask for that raise? Who am I to ask for

her hand in marriage? Who am I to go to college and earn a degree? So many great adventures are never happening because we can't get past "Who am I?"

But God didn't hear his words and say, "You are right, I have the wrong person." God saw something in Moses that he didn't see himself. He saw the potential and calling on his life. He saw who Moses would be if he would trust Him in the process. All around the world, there are people walking miles to find water above ground. Water that is easier to have access to or the only body of water they know. However, it can be perilous to get to the water source, as ferocious animals use the same watering hole. People walk miles and miles with buckets on their heads to bring it back safely to their homes. But little do they know that there may be water right under their feet. All it takes is for someone with resources and vision to see what you can see and access what you don't know how to reach, to make life easier and better. Sometimes God will bring us on a journey to dig deeper in our lives, to draw from the source of potential that is within us. Moses saw the journey and destination as an impossible task, while God saw it as a needed process to reach his personal Promised Land.

When God heard the words of Moses asking, "Who am I?" He gave him an amazing response stating, "I am who I am." God is whatever we need in the time of need. He is the healer to the sick and the compass to the lost. He is the Savior for the damned and the restorer of the broken. Moses faith was in his inability to perform, but his strength would be found in God's ability to transform his life. "I am who I am" should have been Moses' stamp of approval to trust God every single step. As you take inventory of your life, counting up your ability to do what God has commissioned you to do, make sure you add, "I am who I am" to the equation. He is the zero that is multiped by your excuses that cancels them all out.

Moses' Provisions

Exodus 4:1-17

Moses answered, "What if they do not believe me or listen to me and say, 'The Lord did not appear to you'?" [2] *Then the Lord said to him, "What is that in your hand?"*

"A staff," he replied. [3] *The Lord said, "Throw it on the ground." Moses threw it on the ground, and it became a snake, and he ran from it.* [4] *Then the Lord said to him, "Reach out your hand and take it by the tail." So Moses reached out and took hold of the snake and it turned back into a staff in his hand.* [5] *"This," said the Lord, "is so that they may believe that the Lord, the God of their fathers— the God of Abraham, the God of Isaac and the God of Jacob—has appeared to you."* [6] *Then the Lord said, "Put your hand inside your cloak." So Moses put his hand into his cloak, and when he took it out, the skin was leprous—it had become as white as snow.*

[7] *"Now put it back into your cloak," he said. So Moses put his hand back into his cloak, and when he took it out, it was restored, like the rest of his flesh.* [8] *Then the Lord said, "If they do not believe you or pay attention to the first sign, they may believe the second.* [9] *But if they do not believe these two signs or listen to you, take some water from the Nile and pour it on the dry ground. The water you take from the river will become blood on the ground."* [10] *Moses said to the Lord, "Pardon your servant, Lord. I have never been eloquent, neither in the past nor since you have spoken to your servant. I am slow of speech and tongue."* [11] *The Lord said to him, "Who gave human beings their mouths? Who makes them deaf or mute? Who gives them sight or makes them blind? Is it not I, the Lord?* [12] *Now go; I will help you speak and will teach you what to say."* [13] *But Moses said, "Pardon your servant, Lord. Please send someone else."* [14] *Then the Lord's anger burned against Moses and he said, "What about your brother, Aaron the Levite? I know he can speak well.*

He is already on his way to meet you, and he will be glad to see you. ¹⁵ You shall speak to him and put words in his mouth; I will help both of you speak and will teach you what to do. ¹⁶ He will speak to the people for you, and it will be as if he were your mouth and as if you were God to him. ¹⁷ But take this staff in your hand so you can perform the signs with it."

Moses still felt unqualified to start the journey God was sending him on. There were two massive issues that seemed to engulf his attention, which he had a hard time getting past. It might not have seemed like a big deal to others, but for him, it was a wall in the way of him saying yes. He felt powerless to carry out the task, and he believed he didn't speak well enough to articulate the message. God, once again, was trying to get Moses to see He was all he needed. That the very fact that God was calling him was enough to trust Him to start the journey. All the other things would be worked out in the process, as God has a record of being detailed and structured. But at this moment, it wasn't about charts and funds or reports and balances. It was the interviewer and boss asking the question: Would you take the job? Moses felt as if he needed help to do what he was being asked to do, and God provided. When Moses needed to speak, he could rely on his friend and helper named Aaron (whom God referred to as "brother", as we are all family in Christ). When he would speak in front of crowds and people alike, I assume he would whisper in Aaron's ear, and he would proclaim the instructions. Moses felt unqualified to start, so God gave him a tool and helper to get going. Along with his helper, Aaron, God used a staff to aid him to perform the supernatural signs and wonders. But I believe it is essential to know his staff wasn't a magician's wand, waving in the air, chanting spells that caused the signs and wonders, but it was God Himself. The staff was a point of contact and a tool that Moses believe he needed to complete the task.

I firmly believe that even though both of the aids Moses acquired helped him to achieve his goals, they were never the source of his strength to complete them. God was trying to let Moses see once again that "I am who I am" was the motto of his mission. It wasn't possessions that granted Moses power, but his position. His position was that he was standing in authority as a son of God. His power was connected to the God who had commissioned him in the first place. I believe from the start of Moses' life, this was a truth God needed Moses to see. He needed him not to base his qualifications in his own abilities or even others' approval, but to stand on God's promises. He needed him to not rest his faith on what he saw, but what he knew God could and would do. God moved His hands against the Egyptians with ten plagues, all the while teaching Moses that with faith and authority, he could see the hand of God move. It was in the midst of these plagues that God was fathering Moses to transition him from fear to faith. Take a journey with me in the word as Moses found his identity and as a result, his authority in the LORD.

The scenic route

Exodus 7:19-20 (Plague of Blood)
***19** The Lord said to Moses, "Tell Aaron, 'Take your staff and stretch out your hand over the waters of Egypt—over the streams and canals, over the ponds and all the reservoirs—and they will turn to blood.' Blood will be everywhere in, Egypt, even in vessels of wood and stone." **20** Moses and Aaron did just as the Lord had commanded. He raised his staff in the presence of Pharaoh and his officials and struck the water of the Nile, and all the water was changed into blood.*

Exodus 8:5-6 (Plague of Frogs)
5 Then the Lord said to Moses, "Tell Aaron, 'Stretch out your hand with your staff over the streams and canals and ponds, and make frogs come up on the land of Egypt.'" 6 So Aaron stretched out his hand over the waters of Egypt, and the frogs came up and covered the land.

Exodus 8:16-17 (Plague of Gnats)
16 Then the Lord said to Moses, "Tell Aaron, 'Stretch out your staff and strike the dust of the ground,' and throughout the land of Egypt the dust will become gnats." 17 They did this, and when Aaron stretched out his hand with the staff and struck the dust of the ground, gnats came on people and animals. All the dust throughout the land of Egypt became gnats.

In these three passages of scriptures, we can read the interactions Moses had with both Aaron and the staff. Remember these were two tools that Moses had to complete his task. When it was time for Moses to address the crowd, the Lord would speak to Moses to tell Aaron. That was how it went for those three times. But in the next interaction, a massive shift was about to take place. A shift and change that was vital to Moses' future and ministry. An understanding that would help Moses become the mighty man of God we read about today. Moses would smother out the voice of insecurities, turn up the volume of his own faith, and discover his own voice.

Exodus 9:22-23 (Plague of Hail)
*"22 **Then the Lord said to Moses,** "Stretch out your hand toward the sky so that hail will fall all over Egypt—on people and animals and on everything growing in the fields of Egypt." 23 When Moses stretched out his staff toward the sky, the Lord sent thunder and*

hail, and lightning flashed down to the ground. So the Lord rained hail on the land of Egypt;"

Notice the amazing victory in Moses' life as God was no longer asking Moses to tell Aaron, but Moses was speaking to the crowd himself. In spite of the stuttering, lack of eloquent speech or whatever the concern may have been, Moses was vocal about his assignment. He would no longer be bullied in this arena as he was the champion. This was a fact and truth that God was attempting to get him to understand all along; That he had a voice and that he could speak because God was with him.

Aaron did play a significant role to help him in the journey, but he wasn't the reason why he was able to succeed. By no means can Aaron's role be belittled, yet it is important to understand the fact of his involvement. God's desire for Aaron's aid in Moses' life was for him to be a crutch to help him stand and not the power needed to walk. Moses found his voice, and as you read later into his life, it was this very thing that would be needed to help him lead millions of people. If Moses couldn't speak, how would he be able to lead God's people into the Promised Land? As much as the ten plagues were used to free the Hebrews from slavery, they were also used to free Moses from himself.

But the work for God wasn't over yet, as there still was another temporary crutch that God was trying to remove. Just as Moses didn't need Aaron to speak for him, he also didn't need the staff to perform the signs and wonders. Notice from this point on, God was no longer telling Moses to raise up his staff, but his hands. But like before in the journey to Moses' maturity to know God's truth, he struggled a couple of times until he got it. It was not possessions that were granting him the power, but his position in the Lord.

Exodus 10:12-13 (Plague of Locusts)
*12 And the Lord said to Moses, "**Stretch out your hand** over Egypt so that locusts swarm over the land and devour everything growing in the fields, everything left by the hail." 13 So Moses stretched out his staff over Egypt, and the Lord made an east wind blow across the land all that day and all that night. By morning the wind had brought the locusts;*

Right here, you can see God weaning Moses off the crutch of the staff. It wasn't the object or the tool that had the power, but God Himself. Sometimes parents give babies pacifiers to help them self-soothe or aid in other ways. But as the child grows up, they are old enough that they no longer need a pacifier. From some parents' experience, if you yank the pacifier out of their mouths and have them go cold turkey, they will cry, asking for it repeatedly. They truly long for it and deeply believe they need it. But the way to help the child to grow up and mature past their desire for the "sucker" is to give it to the child less often. This interaction isn't for the parents to know the child no longer needs it, they already know. It is for the child to come to the understanding that they no longer need it. Thus, they will start asking for it less and less, and sooner or later they won't ask for it at all.

I grew up in a little town in North Carolina called Eden. I can remember helping my mom in the garden at the side of our house. It was hard manual labor, and my mom loved it. She still has a green thumb to this day and enjoys her time with nature. There was one time that we were planting green beans in the garden when she asked me to do something that left me perplexed. After we planted to green beans, she asked me to put a stick in the ground right near where we planted. I was baffled as to the reason to plant this broken broomstick, but I did it anyway while asking her why. Of course, she wasn't expecting the broomstick to all of a sudden bud and bear fruit, but she placed the stick by the forthcoming vine so it could have a standard to grow on. It didn't make the plant grow, but just gave it a stable place to grow. The staff and Aaron's involvement weren't what made Moses grow, but became the standard that aided in his growth. From the beginning of the story of the plagues, God was attempting to father Moses and wean him from the crutch of the staff. Once again, not because God needed to know if Moses needed it or not, but for Moses to understand that he didn't.

Exodus 10:21-22 (Plague of Darkness)
***21** Then the Lord said to Moses, "**Stretch out your hand** toward the sky so that darkness spreads over Egypt—darkness that can be felt." **22** So **Moses stretched out his hand** toward the sky, and total darkness covered all Egypt for three days*

Yes! Moses got it. He pushed the fear out of the way and understood the lesson that God was trying to teach him all along. Here we can finally read where both tools that Moses believed he needed to carry out his assignment were removed. God was speaking to Moses directly, and he was addressing everyone for Him. To add to the victory, when God instructed Moses to stretch out his hands, he no longer stretched out his staff, but his hands. Moses understood the life-changing revelation, it wasn't the possessions that granted him power, but his position found in God. How radical can your life become if you come to the same revelation in your life? The things and people you have been waiting for to qualify you to dream are no longer on your waiting list to start. If you read from the end of Moses' life to the beginning of his commission moment at the burning bush, this was a lesson that marked his life. A lesson that the word of God reminds us of so powerfully in the book of Romans.

Romans 8:31
"What, then, shall we say in response to these things? If God is for us, who can be against us?"

Secure in his security

After the final plague happened, Pharaoh let God's people go. They left celebrating that they no longer had to be in bondage. They could live and worship freely without the chains of slavery. As they left Egypt, the Israelites took everything they owned with them as well as plunder from their oppressors. God sent a cloud to guide them during the day and a pillar of fire to lead them during the night. However, the smiles soon turned to frowns, and the laughter into crying. As they journeyed to their Promised Land, Pharaoh changed his mind and gathered up his army and pursued the former slaves. They approached the Red Sea, turned around and saw their former captors. People were going crazy and losing hope. They blamed Moses for their current state and were extremely upset. Can you image how Moses would have felt if God didn't mature Moses to understand his position found in God? This could have been a time in which his worries, doubt, and insecurities would have overwhelmed him, but that was far from the case. The same voice that used to be shaky with doubt, addressed the crowd with boldness and certainty.

Exodus 14:13-14
"Moses answered the people, "Do not be afraid. Stand firm and you will see the deliverance the Lord will bring you today. The Egyptians you see today you will never see again. 14 The Lord will fight for you; you need only to be still."

Another remarkable moment in history was about to take place in Moses' life. He faced two challenges once again, something that didn't make sense in his own eyes. God was about to split the Red Sea and use Moses as an instrument to do it. But pay close attention to the instructions that our Heavenly Father gave Moses and Moses' response. God was about to give Moses another chance to re-instill his convictions. God told him to raise his staff and stretch out his hands, but Moses simply stretched out his hands.

Exodus 14:16;21
16 Raise your staff and stretch out your hand over the sea to divide the water so that the Israelites can go through the sea on dry ground. 21 Then Moses stretched out his hand over the sea, and all that night the Lord drove the sea back with a strong east wind and turned it into dry land. The waters were divided

Moses understood that God was making the difference in his life. It was not what he had or didn't have, but who he was. He stretched out his hands, and a mighty wind blew until they were able to walk on dry ground. The Hebrews crossed to the other side, safe and sound, seeing the incredible power God had. This became an encounter that would mark the Israelites forever. Of all the people God could have used to do this, He choose a person who was scared to take the first step because insecurities told him to stay put.

Exodus 14:26-27
26 Then the Lord said to Moses, "Stretch out your hand over the sea so that the waters may flow back over the Egyptians and their chariots and horsemen." 27 Moses stretched out his hand over the sea, and at daybreak the sea went back to its place. The Egyptians were fleeing toward it, and the Lord swept them into the sea.

Your voice and staff

There is a Moses complex in all of us that we must face and confront. This battle of "I can, and I can't" is a real struggle that can no longer be undermined. God took Moses on a journey through a series of events for him to understand that he could do what God had called him to do. He had a voice, and he had access to the strength and power to achieve the goals. Are you in a season in your life where you are struggling as Moses did? Is there a dream inside of you that is always in the forefront of your mind, but insecurities are telling you that you will never be able to do it? It is important that you come to the same understanding Moses came to. The same God who walked with Moses every step of the way also walks with us today. No more excuses as to why you can't start or dream. Stop allowing yourself to be the thing you keep tripping over. You have a voice, and you have the strength to stand.

There is a well-known saying, "How do you eat an elephant?" The answer is: "One bite at a time." It is the same in life, but you will never take the bite if you feel that you are unqualified even to open your mouth. Your time is now, and this is your chance.

What would have happened if Moses ran away after his experience with the burning bush? Moses' obedience to his purpose was directly connected to the freedom of an entire generation. Your "yes" to God and your assignment can benefit the lives of people you aren't even aware of. The time is now for you to overcome the internal battle and stand over the carcass of fear. Your future is waiting on you. Please don't miss your appointment because insecurities are attempting to make you late. This is your chance!

CHAPTER 7
DESERTS AND MOUNTAINS

A harsh reality of life is that you cannot always take all the people in your past into your future. You may have great intentions, but as time goes on, people grow in different directions. It is the fear of losing and downsizing that oftentimes keeps us in our place. It's an emotional battle because you don't want to seem ungrateful and have your advancement be viewed in a negative way. Maybe you put yourself on a guilt trip, moving out of the rough part of town to a gated community. Maybe after you graduated from college and started your career, you didn't have evenings and weekends off. Now your friends are telling you that you are acting "uppity" or as if you are too good for them, when in fact your schedule has shifted. Perhaps you are out of high school, and you get married. You can't spend all your free time with your friends and need to invest in your marriage. Now they are telling you that you have changed and don't care about them anymore, when in fact you are trying to learn how to live under the new boundaries in your life.

You may have been known as a party animal and would go to the club every weekend. You slept around, got wasted, and were addicted to drugs, but your life changed when you encountered God. You gave your life to Jesus and decided to turn your life around; you got clean and told yourself that you are going to save yourself for marriage. Due to your desire not to place yourself in tempting situations, you tell your friends you aren't going clubbing anymore. But their response to you is that you think you are too good, you're judging them or acting "holier than thou." Do you compromise on your convictions and throw your goals down the toilet? No, you stick to them and encourage them to understand. If they refuse to support you, then the hard truth is that there may need to be a change in your circle of influence. There are countless examples of moments when the dynamics of life bring moments when change must happen. If I gave you a pad and pen, you could personally write down many moments in your life when you were at crossroads, having to make similar choices.

A massive reason why people are petrified of seizing their chances are the people and possessions they must let go of. Yet all throughout the word of God, we see examples of how the Lord used deserts to remove people and ideologies from people's lives. If they were going to get in their Promised Lands, there were things and mindsets they were not allowed to take with them. We all want the experiences and joys that come from a mountaintop view. But the struggle in the valleys and deserts is the passageway to get there. Your desert will teach you lessons that your mountaintop never could.

Mirages

Many life-changing things happened in deserts during biblical times. The deserts were not only a place that people traveled through, but was a place of incredible life lessons. It was a harsh climate that you couldn't lackadaisically saunter through. Alarming degrees of temperature, from destructive heat to polar cold can both happen in those moments. Moses, Caleb, Joshua, and the Israelites experienced lessons in a desert and wilderness that shifted the perspectives of all the parties involved. Sometime after the Lord delivered the Israelites out of Egyptian slavery, the Lord gave Moses simple instructions regarding the next step to take. God had a Promised Land in mind in Canaan, but asked them to explore it. All He was asking for was a report of the area and for Moses to confirm with the people how amazing the land was. It was fertile, rich, and prosperous, perfect for the Israelites to establish and settle down. But just like anything in life, they came back with different outlooks. Two different reports were shared with Moses and the rest of the people of Israel. A report of fear and impossibilities and a report of faith, excitement, and courage.

Numbers 13:17-33
17 When Moses sent them to explore Canaan, he said, "Go up through the Negev and on into the hill country. 18 See what the land is like and whether the people who live there are strong or weak, few or many. 19 What kind of land do they live in? Is it good or bad? What kind of towns do they live in? Are they unwalled or fortified? 20 How is the soil? Is it fertile or poor? Are there trees in it or not? Do your best to bring back some of the fruit of the land." (It was the season for the first ripe grapes.) 21 So they went up and explored the land from the Desert of Zin as far as Rehob, toward Lebo Hamath. 22 They went up through the Negev and came to Hebron, where Ahiman, Sheshai and Talmai, the descendants of Anak, lived. (Hebron had been built seven years before Zoan in Egypt.) 23 When they reached the Valley of Eshkol, they cut off a branch bearing a single cluster of grapes. Two of them carried it on a pole between them, along with some pomegranates and figs. 24 That place was called the Valley of Eshkol because of the cluster of grapes the Israelites cut off there. 25 At the end of forty days they returned from exploring the land. 26 They came back to Moses and Aaron and the whole Israelite community at Kadesh in the Desert of Paran. There they reported to them and to the whole assembly and showed them the fruit of the land. 27 They gave Moses

*this account: "We went into the land to which you sent us, and it does flow with milk and honey! Here is its fruit. ²⁸ But the people who live there are powerful, and the cities are fortified and very large. We even saw descendants of Anak there. ²⁹ The Amalekites live in the Negev; the Hittites, Jebusites and Amorites live in the hill country; and the Canaanites live near the sea and along the Jordan." ³⁰ Then Caleb silenced the people before Moses and said, "We should go up and take possession of the land, for **we can certainly do it.**" ³¹ But the men who had gone up with him said, "We can't attack those people; they are stronger than we are." ³² And they spread among the Israelites a bad report about the land they had explored. They said, "The land we explored devours those living in it. All the people we saw there are of great size. ³³ We saw the Nephilim there (the descendants of Anak come from the Nephilim). We seemed like grasshoppers in our own eyes, and we looked the same to them."*

It is amazing how, when we solely see a problem, we can act out the next series of events. It is like we make ourselves superheroes with the power to predict precisely how the future is going to happen. We can see an obstacle that is in between us and our goal and talk ourselves out of it. You won't see eye-to-eye with everyone in your life, and I know you aren't surprised about that. Not everyone will be your cheerleaders or your supporters. You may not have the crowd shouting out your name like at a professional sporting event.

The small group of spies came back with a report to give to Moses as well as a sample of the harvest of the land. They confirmed how great a land it was and how it was fertile and suitable for living. After all, this was the place that God had in mind for His people all along. Like a sudden U-turn in a busy street, fear was about to spread to the travelers on the journey to the Promised Land. One side gave Moses a favorable report of how the land is ready for them but would require effort. The other side saw the journey to their promise as impossible because there were giants in the land. For them, the risk wasn't worth the reward, and they grumbled and complained, causing mental sickness to spread throughout the camp. Their tongues were the needles injecting fear and disbelief in the ears of those around them. An outbreak was taking place, and just like any infectious disease, quarantine needed to take place.

Caleb silenced the people in front of Moses, to stop the contagious negative words and outlook, but it had already taken root in the minds of the listeners. They continued to speak death and despair about the dynamics of the situation, discussing how large the giants and enemies were in the land, as if God hadn't shown His mighty hands to them many times. They witnessed the cloud by day and the pillar of fire by night. They saw the water turn into blood and boils appear on the skins of their oppressors. They saw the Red Sea split and their oppressors swallowed up in it, yet with what they had already experienced, they still struggled with the issue before them. It seemed like none of that mattered because they couldn't get past how they saw themselves. They saw themselves as grasshoppers, and like fear, they believed a colossal lie. They made an assumption about the enemies that they hadn't experienced for themselves; they believed they looked the same to their enemies. Regardless of the size difference, it wouldn't have mattered. Moses didn't send them on a stroll through enemy territory, taking pictures of the scenery like a tourist. It was God's intent to fight for them, and when that happens, it doesn't matter your size. Just look at ask David's life.

Numbers 14:1-11
14 That night all the members of the community raised their voices and wept aloud. ² All the Israelites grumbled against Moses and Aaron, and the whole assembly said to them, "If only we had died in Egypt! Or in this wilderness! ³ Why is the Lord bringing us to

this land only to let us fall by the sword? Our wives and children will be taken as plunder. Wouldn't it be better for us to go back to Egypt?"⁴ And they said to each other, "We should choose a leader and go back to Egypt." ⁵ Then Moses and Aaron fell facedown in front of the whole Israelite assembly gathered there. ⁶ Joshua son of Nun and Caleb son of Jephunneh, who were among those who had explored the land, tore their clothes ⁷ and said to the entire Israelite assembly, "The land we passed through and explored is exceedingly good. ⁸ If the Lord is pleased with us, he will lead us into that land, a land flowing with milk and honey, and will give it to us. ⁹ Only do not rebel against the Lord. And do not be afraid of the people of the land, because we will devour them. Their protection is gone, but the Lord is with us. Do not be afraid of them."¹⁰ But the whole assembly talked about stoning them. Then the glory of the Lord appeared at the tent of meeting to all the Israelites. ¹¹ The Lord said to Moses, "How long will these people treat me with contempt? How long will they refuse to believe in me, in spite of all the signs I have performed among them?

This passage of scripture is so real, and I firmly believe hits home with many of us. The Israelites grumbled and complained against the leadership that God had set in place. Beyond that, they began to question the actions that God had taken due to their current situation. The icing on the cake is that they were willing to go back as slaves, under the captivity of the Egyptians, rather than to navigate into the waters God had foreseen. They would rather experience the fist of a master, the oppression of a people group, than to fight forward to a place that God had prepared for them. Yet again, it is remarkable to read such a thing, but there truly is nothing new under the sun. How many times have we heard or read a promise of God and shouted about it, yet stopped contending for it? Our carnal nature and self-soothing habits and addictions will always be our default. When the reset button of our efforts is pressed by fear and frustration, we will end up doing the same old things, with the same old stuff with the same old people.

Maybe during stressful times, you used to grab a cigarette or blunt to relax. You were doing good and had been clean for so long, but you got bad news, and it was easier to smoke a substance to calm down than to methodically work through the emotions. You just got out of a bad, abusive, and toxic relationship that you swore up and down you would never get back into. It was easier at first because you had a support system in place that held you accountable. You changed your number so they couldn't text you anymore, making a commitment that you were waiting and preparing yourself for the right one. But time passed by and you got tired of opening your Instagram, seeing other people getting engaged. You wanted to be happy for them, but the nagging thought is in the back of your mind, saying, "When is my chance?" Months pass by, and loneliness is trying to bombard you with lies that you will always be alone. In desperation, you slide into that ex "DM" and shoot your shot. Y'all get back together with the hopes that things will be different, only to discover they are exactly the same. Why? Because y'all didn't take the time to work on yourselves individually, which continued the chaos that you swore you would avoid.

Yet you settle for the lie that this is the best you can do, making a choice to go back into the same bondage that you used to praise God you were out off. Now when anyone is saying that your relationship isn't healthy, you call them a hater and jealous. The same voices that carried you through your moments of hardships are now the same voices you curse for being judgmental. You update your social media with a verse completely taken out of context, with the hashtag, "Only God can judge me." Does any of this hit close to home? Have you backed away from your convictions, goals, and dreams because of fear?

Like an STD, the disease of fear and doubt was transmitted through auditory contact as it pleased the flesh. Gossip was the fire that consumed open ears and yielding tongues. Once again, Joshua and Caleb attempted to stop the malignant tumor from making its way to affect the entire body. They echoed the overwhelming truth that God was going to fight for them, but the rest of the people didn't want to hear it. So much so, that they all talked about stoning Joshua and Caleb. It is sad that the quickest voices to be killed off in the lives of a person in error are the ones attempting to help them the most.

You have roaches

Numbers 14:20-35
20 The Lord replied, "I have forgiven them, as you asked. 21 Nevertheless, as surely as I live and as surely as the glory of the Lord fills the whole earth, 22 not one of those who saw my glory and the signs I performed in Egypt and in the wilderness but who disobeyed me and tested me ten times— 23 not one of them will ever see the land I promised on oath to their ancestors. No one who has treated me with contempt will ever see it. 24 But because my servant Caleb has a different spirit and follows me wholeheartedly, I will bring him into the land he went to, and his descendants will inherit it. 25 Since the Amalekites and the Canaanites are living in the valleys, turn back tomorrow and set out toward the desert along the route to the Red Sea." 26 The Lord said to Moses and Aaron: 27 "How long will this wicked community grumble against me? I have heard the complaints of these grumbling Israelites. 28 So tell them, 'As surely as I live, declares the Lord, I will do to you the very thing I heard you say: 29 In this wilderness your bodies will fall—every one of you twenty years old or more who was counted in the census and who has grumbled against me. 30 Not one of you

will enter the land I swore with uplifted hand to make your home, except Caleb son of Jephunneh and Joshua son of Nun. ³¹ As for your children that you said would be taken as plunder, I will bring them in to enjoy the land you have rejected. ³² But as for you, your bodies will fall in this wilderness.³³ Your children will be shepherds here for forty years, suffering for your unfaithfulness, until the last of your bodies lies in the wilderness. ³⁴ For forty years—one year for each of the forty days you explored the land—you will suffer for your sins and know what it is like to have me against you.' ³⁵ I, the Lord, have spoken, and I will surely do these things to this whole wicked community, which has banded together against me. They will meet their end in this wilderness; here they will die."

The harsh reality is that our words will get us in trouble and in places that we can't get ourselves out of. After everything they went through, they would not be allowed to go in the Promised Land. In fact, God told Moses to turn everyone around, and they circled around in the wilderness, not with a destination in mind but with a goal. All the people who had the stinking thinking had to be removed from the equation. The desert and wilderness that God took them through became a sifting process that left them lighter but brighter. When all is said and done, the only ones left would be Moses, Caleb, Joshua. As hard as this is to believe, the LORD knew He had to clean house. Even though they were physically freed from slavery, they were still thinking in bondage. God had to turn the plane around and put it in a holding pattern until it was safe to land. There was baggage in the minds of the unbelieving and lazy that couldn't be taken into the Promised Land. They had roaches in their homes, which breed quicker than you can spray them. If God didn't deal with the infestation, there would be an invitation to the same mindset in their new home. In the land flowing with milk and honey, roaches would be coming out of the baggage and lifestyle that they didn't clean out.

When you are stepping out into your promise, you will at some point experience the same kind of separation. The truth of the matter is that there are some people, mindsets, and behaviors that don't belong in your present day. Sadly, it is the struggle of not wanting to let go because we feel we owe our yesterday for where we are today. But there is a difference between being thankful and being indebted. God uses deserts to bring people into your life and remove people from your life. Complaining, gossip, slander, and other toxic behaviors will destroy anything they touch, including your hopes and dreams.

When the Wright brothers chose to build an airplane and fly, there were changes along the way. They had to read the signs around them and know when it was time to leave Dayton, OH, to move to a place better suited to their goals and dreams. The inventors moved to Kitty Hawk, NC, where the ground was softer, and the wind gusts were stronger. Their success demanded a radical move away from what they were accustomed to, and to a place that was a custom fit to their desires, goals, and purpose. There is nothing wrong with staying put where you grew up and making a life for yourself, if that is your goal and passion. There is nothing wrong with having an average job and making ends meet if that is your wish in life. But if you have a dream within you and you are not moving forward in it, you are both robbing yourself and stealing from your legacy. Like a miner panning for gold, God had to sift through the Israelites and remove, through their own actions, those who didn't belong.

Yes, it is easy to shake our heads at the Israelites and think, "How can they think such a thing?" But we shouldn't be so quick to throw stones when we have been collecting them from the same river. How many times has God shown Himself faithful in your life?

How many times have you prayed to God to work a situation out, and He did? How many miracles have you tracked down, with Him showing up and showing off?

However, standing in the wake of another chance for God to get the glory in the hard dynamics of our lives, we struggle with the notion that He will do it again. His power doesn't have limits or need to be recharged. He has enough grace and strength to pour out on everyone. But like the Israelites, we tend to forget when fear is looking us directly in the face. As if fear was holding their puppet strings, they danced with uncertainty under the lights of doom and gloom, giving every viewer a show. A mirage was taking place right there in the desert. They didn't see things correctly, and they needed a fresh vision. They looked in the mirror and saw themselves as grasshoppers, just insects compared to the hardships that awaited them in the future of their journey. Sometimes you must leave the naysayers behind. The people looking at themselves as grasshoppers had already lost the battle. What is sad is that some people will assume that the limits they placed upon themselves are the parameters and regulations that they have to live by. They will tell you it can't be done because they tried it before. The same, with good intentions, tell you it is impossible because it didn't work out for them. News flash: you aren't them, and they may not have had the same tools to work with as you do.

Beware of the other spies who see the same opportunity as you do and assume that failure is also in your future. What Caleb and Joshua saw was a bright future while the others saw dark days ahead. It is frustrating when you see people throw away their potential because effort is required to step into their purpose. Resistance isn't always a

> Resistance isn't always a sign that you are moving in the wrong direction. It could be the pressure you feel as you are scaling up your mountain.

sign that you are moving in the wrong direction. It could be the pressure you feel as you are scaling up your mountain.

Hardships

In the classroom of life, the exam that hardships are placing on your desk is a test everyone has to take. Hard times happen to everyone, whether you believe you are doing everything right or you know you are making mistakes. There is a difference between "Life happening to you" and "You happening to life." There are some situations that we find ourselves in that may be out of our control. A health scare, your boss downsizing, or a car accident can completely change a person's life. These are examples of life happening to you, but the other side of the coin may be the fruit of our own labor. Addictions, lack of self-control, the refusal to get on a budget can push your life rolling downhill. Your spouse told you countless times to change your habits, but you didn't listen, assuming that they would always be there.

One day on your way home from work, you pull up in the driveway, noticing that her car isn't there. You open the door to a quiet house with a note on the table. Written on the paper are words that cut you deeply: "I told you to choose either the alcohol or me and you chose to drink, it's over." Now you are eating from the fruit of your own labor, alone with regret and guilt keeping you company.

It is crucial that we draw this clear line of understanding before you go any further. If we don't look in the mirror and examine the reasons why we may be in the place we are at in life, we will repeat the same behaviors that got us there in the first place. My book, *Crowns are Greater Than Trophies* will be an excellent aid for you to break the cycle of behaviors that are robbing you. It is imperative that a moment of introspection happens, because if we don't take inventory of the hard times we are in, we will stay there. The hardest moments in your life can bring out the most profound lessons. We must gain the wisdom and knowledge to know which kind of desert we are in.

Taking a sharp turn from eating the fruits of our own mistakes is a lesson we will learn in life along the way. It's like an RPG (role-playing game) video game. As you play it, and the longer you stay in the game, the more upgrades you get. If we become so frustrated at one level and press the power button to quit, we will never win. God uses the circumstances of life to bring us to a level of maturity that prepares us to win. He may not be the author of your pain or the reason for your hardships, but He won't waste a moment to teach you a lesson that will aid you in your life.

James 1:2-5
2 Consider it pure joy, my brothers and sisters, whenever you face trials of many kinds, 3 because you know that the testing of your faith produces perseverance. 4 Let perseverance finish its work so that you may be mature and complete, not lacking anything. 5 If any of you lacks wisdom, you should ask God, who gives generously to all without finding fault, and it will be given to you.

Don't throw in the towel because the ones who started the race with you have already quit running. Don't stop studying because some untrusted voice is telling you that it isn't worth it. Do you stop believing in yourself because someone told you that you couldn't? Please, I beg you, don't stop believing because you feel you are alone. Your desert will teach you things that your mountaintop never could. The mountaintop is a destination, but it is the journey that matures us to arrive there in the first place. So, if you are frustrated because people don't believe in your dreams or tell you all the reasons why you out of all people can't do it, don't quit because of negative words spoken. Seek wise counsel and make an educated plan to achieve your dreams. Find trusted people who know what they are talking about, and not the troll on social media hating on you because you are trying. This is your chance and you shouldn't waste it waiting for everyone to support you and believe you can do it. After all, they may only see themselves as grasshoppers, but you know you are more than that.

You are a child of a king with royal blood flowing through your veins. You are a child of God, filled with the Spirit's power, walking in an understanding that you are not fighting alone. You are cherished, valued, and believed in by the creator of the heavens and Earth. You aren't an oops or regret, and God didn't place this dream within you to dangle it in front of your face. No, it was placed there to motivate you towards your purpose. Whatever it may be, your promise awaits you, but you may have to walk through some deserts. Get your bugout bag ready and be prepared at a moment's notice when destiny knocks on your door. Gather your water, sunblock, and your survival kit as you traverse through the harsh climate of expectations and hardships. Make sure every step has sure footing, so you don't slip down and quit the climb. Get ready, because this is your chance.

CHAPTER 8
P.R.O.C.E.S.S

In the last few chapters, I have addressed the sleeping giants that have been blocking your way to your goals, from fears, excuses, obstacles, losing relationships, and other real-life issues. I hope that at this point you have made a deep dive in your past and present actions to see if you have been your greatest hindrance. It doesn't feel great when we discover that all this time, the greatest enemy to our dreams was the one dreaming them in the first place. We can trip up on our own two feet, attempting to move forward in life, yet wondering why we aren't making forward progress. The vinegar to the baking soda that causes us to erupt inside in the pursuit of our goals is frustration. It's a burning flame that consumes us from the inside out. It affects our clarity of vision and ushers in a cloudy mind.

Frustrations make small issues larger; they will make a small deal a big deal and blow it up out of proportion. When you are frustrated, it can seem like every little inconvenience is the end of the world. Yet it is critical that we never allow frustration to give us permission to quit. Frustration is an emotion with slippery handles, as it is hard to get a grasp on it when it is leading the way. It is like a drunk person making bad decisions at the bar or hotel, waking up to a random person but not remembering what they had done. Frustration, if allowed to drive, will breed and fester in our hearts and take control, either parking the vehicle of our lives in regret or driving off a cliff and taking your legacy with it. We, people, are led by frustration, emotional suicide bombers making innocent bystanders victims because they said an unknown word that triggered us. Frustration can kill a career, destroy a family, and pollute a dream. Which begs the question: Why are people frustrated? Have people thrown in the towel and yelled, "I quit," when they just got started or have been trying for a lengthy period of time? Of course. I firmly believe when you pull down all the layers that are covering frustration, you will discover control right in the middle.

We are creatures of control, and we thrive on the notion of regularity. Consistency can bring security, and that gives birth to peace of mind. We want all our ducks in a row and to be able to play connect the dots from point A to B and from B to C. We want to see not only the end result, but every step along the way, and be aware of all the surprises. The feeling of not being in control will rev the engine of frustration to alarming rates. The isolation that occurs because you don't know what to do, or the steps before you don't make any sense, can feel overwhelming. We know that God is in control, and He will open doors that can't be shut and shut doors that can't be opened.

The frustrations that happen in the hallways deflate the motivation to continue the journey. It is the length from the process to the promise that adds to the difficult expedition. But in God's cookbook, the recipe that He oftentimes uses to makes dreams come true is a process. Whenever God gives a promise, it goes hand-in-hand with a process. Oh, you want to be healed, go wash in the Jordan river seven times. Joseph had a dream of leadership when he was young, but endured a series of events that looked nothing like his vision. He was thrown into a pit, sold into slavery, and placed in jail accused of a sexual harassment crime that he didn't even commit. But hindsight is 20/20, and at the time in his life that he was finally standing in that place of power and leadership, he said some powerful words.

Genesis 50:20
"You intended to harm me, but God intended it for good to accomplish what is now being done, the saving of many lives."

Butterfly

It is the lack of understanding God's plan when we are walking along the path to our purpose that we can wrongly use as permission to quit. When God gives a promise, it is a three-legged race tied to your process. We understand the importance of "process" in many other areas of life, but struggle with it in our own lives. In order to eat the cake, it needs to be prepared and baked. It's not just having the eggs, flour, and sugar before you that makes the cake. If you just have the ingredients, then you only have potential. But to shift from potential to results, the hot flames of the process are vital. Your process is the incubator that prepares you for hatching and developing. The animal kingdom is remarkable and gives amazing life illustrations that highlight many truths in life.

When a caterpillar goes into a cocoon, it is undergoing a process of transformation. This process can't be rushed in any way, or it will kill the would-be butterfly. If I wanted to help the butterfly out and cut a slit into the cocoon so it would have an easier time breaking out, I would be doing more harm than good. Why? Because it is the very process of breaking out of the cocoon that strengthens the butterfly's wings so it can fly later. If I interfere with the process by trying to impose my own will, I would be robbing the creature of its intended purpose and potential. We can't abort the process, looking for the easy way out.

Whatever your dreams, goals, and aspirations may be, there will be required steps to take. If a degree is needed to get your dream job, then you are going to have to walk through the process of going to college. When you get frustrated while you are taking courses that you have no interest in, or the stress of the exams drive you crazy, you must not quit. Whether you just got married or have been married for a while, and you go into a hard season, don't give up on each other. Whatever that dream is in your life that you keep talking about, it is going to require a journey that may not always feel pleasant. Sometimes the pathway is hard, and even at times it simply doesn't make sense.

Proverbs 3:5-6
"Trust in the Lord with all your heart and lean not on your own understanding; ⁶ in all your ways submit to him, and he will make your paths straight."

Understanding Frustration

The word of God is bursting at the seams with examples of when God, the Lord, instructed mankind to do things that didn't make sense. A great example of this is the story of Joshua and the walls of Jericho.

Joshua 6:1-16
6 "Now the gates of Jericho were securely barred because of the Israelites. No one went out and no one came in. ² Then the Lord said to Joshua, "See, I have delivered Jericho into your hands, along with its king and its fighting men. ³ March around the city once with all the armed men. Do this for six days. ⁴ Have seven priests carry trumpets of rams' horns in front of the ark. On the seventh day, march around the city seven times, with the priests

blowing the trumpets. ⁵ *When you hear them sound a long blast on the trumpets, have the whole army give a loud shout; then the wall of the city will collapse and the army will go up, everyone straight in."* ⁶ *So Joshua son of Nun called the priests and said to them, "Take up the ark of the covenant of the Lord and have seven priests carry trumpets in front of it."* ⁷ *And he ordered the army, "Advance! March around the city, with an armed guard going ahead of the ark of the Lord."* ⁸ *When Joshua had spoken to the people, the seven priests carrying the seven trumpets before the Lord went forward, blowing their trumpets, and the ark of the Lord's covenant followed them.* ⁹ *The armed guard marched ahead of the priests who blew the trumpets, and the rear guard followed the ark. All this time the trumpets were sounding.* ¹⁰ *But Joshua had commanded the army, "Do not give a war cry, do not raise your voices, do not say a word until the day I tell you to shout. Then shout!"* ¹¹ *So he had the ark of the Lord carried around the city, circling it once. Then the army returned to camp and spent the night there.* ¹² *Joshua got up early the next morning and the priests took up the ark of the Lord.* ¹³ *The seven priests carrying the seven trumpets went forward, marching before the ark of the Lord and blowing the trumpets. The armed men went ahead of them and the rear guard followed the ark of the Lord, while the trumpets kept sounding.* ¹⁴ *So on the second day they marched around the city once and returned to the camp. They did this for six days.* ¹⁵ *On the seventh day, they got up at daybreak and marched around the city seven times in the same manner, except that on that day they circled the city seven times.* ¹⁶ *The seventh time around, when the priests sounded the trumpet blast, Joshua commanded the army, "Shout! For the Lord has given you the city!"*

Joshua 6:20

"When the trumpets sounded, the army shouted, and at the sound of the trumpet, when the men gave a loud shout, the wall collapsed; so everyone charged straight in, and they took the city."

God gave Joshua and the Israelites a promise and a process. The promise was that He was giving them the land that they saw before them. However, the process was for them to march around the city seven times and give a massive shout. I can imagine the bewilderment on the faces of the Israelites as Joshua gave the instructions, maybe thinking to themselves, "Is that it?" They didn't have a catapult or other large weaponry that would make sense. All they had was instructions from God, and if they thought that it wasn't enough, they maybe would have left the endeavor altogether. A huge point in this story is seeing how Joshua added additional instructions that God didn't ask him to do. Yes, he was obedient to the other details. But he told the Israelites to stay silent, not to speak or even say a word until they heard the sound of the trumpet. I believe that was wisdom on his part, as they had an extensive history of robbing themselves of a breakthrough and a victory because of the toxic words, slander, and gossip spewing out of their mouths. Marching around a fortress with weaponry, trumpets, obedience, and the ark of the covenant, which held the presence of God, must have been a powerful sight to see. They had to walk in a level of trust outside of what they saw and stand on what they knew. This was the same God who parted the Red Sea and freed them from Egypt. This was the same God who knew it all, so they just had to trust in God's record of success. They needed to encourage themselves knowing if God gave the promise, they must be obedient to the process. Sure enough, just like every other time that they made the shift from their own understanding to an act of faith, God made a way. The seventh time around, they shouted and the walls fell down.

Scriptures are filled with story after story of people who trusted God during a journey that was hard to understand. God is such an amazing administrator that He doesn't only have your destination in mind, but the transformation that will occur during the journey. Are you going to trust God during the times that you don't understand? I am by no means suggesting that we stop thinking, dreaming, and planning, as they are also vital things to do to be successful. We must cultivate a sharp mind that thinks ahead and is strategic. But there will be a time when you just don't know what to do or where to go, when you are so frustrated in your journey that you just have to stand on His Word. The hardest moments in your life are the times when you are walking through your valley. The toughest moments can happen when the zeal is fading away, and the joy seems hard to muster up. Whatever season you may be in your life as you run towards your prize, do not lose heart and do not quit.

Galatians 6:9
"Let us not become weary in doing good, for at the proper time we will reap a harvest if we do not give up."

The word "weary" means to lose strength, energy, and excitement for something or a task. It also means to become impatient, which is very easy to do. During your specific process and during your time of need, don't grow weary. Remember to be patient and make up in your mind that you are here for the long haul. Your harvest is coming, and your degree is on the way. Your healing is just around the corner, and your business is about to pull up at any moment. Here is an acronym that will aid you as you are fighting frustration while continuing moving towards your goals.

P.R.O.C.E.S.S is:
Patience
Remembrance
Obedience
Concentration
Encouragement
Supplication and
Strength.

Patience

We want things yesterday while it is still today. It is vital that we learn how to take things one day at the time. Impatience can encourage you to rush things and do a sloppy job. If you are cooking food and the stove needs to be on medium, putting the flame on high isn't going to cause it to cook faster but just burn the food. When we are impatient, we can become nasty, selfish, and aggressive people all because we aren't getting want we want when we want. If you need any indication of this, just go to the grocery store when they only have a few registers open. People will have attitudes with the cashier and then turn to the people in front of and behind them, trying to add bystanders into the pity party that they are throwing. Impatience looks for shortcuts and loopholes, which isn't seeking the maturity of the journey, just the end result. We need the fruit of the Spirit consistently yielding a harvest in our lives.

Galatians 5:22-23
"But the fruit of the Spirit is love, joy, peace, forbearance, kindness, goodness, faithfulness, 23 gentleness, and self-control..."

Remembrance

Remembrance creates a focal point, a place to put your sights upon that feeds the "why" behind what you are trying to accomplish. It's essential to have a healthy sight picture so you can hit your mark and target. When shooting a firearm, having a clear sight picture is important for obvious reasons. When holding up a handgun and shooting further out, it becomes hard to see a little target. But what you are supposed to do is align your front and rear sights, take aim, but focus on your front sight. What happens is amazing because both your rear sight and the target in front of you become blurry, but your front sight is clear. With the correct grip and trigger pull, you will be able to hit your target with ease with the first shot. An added issue occurs with the follow-up shot due to the recoil, which gets you out of alignment for a brief moment. It is at this point that you have to go through the same steps so you can hit the target again.

Remembering what you are aiming at is vital as you are walking, fighting, and contending for your dreams. It's easy to drop the ball and forget the race if you become distracted by the flash from the muzzle or the recoil that life will always bring your way. You started your business and hit your first speed bump. Do you throw the entire LLC down the drain or pick the dream back up, take aim and shoot for it again? Remember what you are contending for during the frustrations of your process.

Obedience

Obedience is a hard thing to do sometimes because it requires a level of submission that we aren't always willing to give. Maybe you have a coach who has been to the place that you are trying to go. Maybe you have a board of advisors giving you sound wisdom that will land you a client that will take you to the next level. Maybe it is the diet plan from the personal trainer that gave you clear guidelines of what to eat and when to eat. Whatever the case may be, follow the guidance of qualified people, mentors, and coaches who can take you to your goals. Have you ever done something wrong, that you knew was an error while you were committing the act? Have you ever ignored God's instructions, and like the lost younger son you desired to live life without accountability? How many times did it turn around and bite you? Jesus has your best interests in mind, and you need to keep that in mind.

Proverbs 12:1
"Whoever loves discipline loves knowledge, but whoever hates correction is stupid."

Concentration

Concentration demands attention and focus, which many things and people around you are also asking for. When you become dedicated to your goals, dreams, and mission, there will need to be some sacrifices along the way. I don't believe you should ever lay your spouse and children on the altar of ambition, because you will also lose what's most important. But there will be times that you won't be able to go out on the town with your friends because you need to study for the upcoming exam. Maybe you shouldn't go out to that expensive restaurant because you are saving up to purchase a house. An aspect that makes concentration so hard is that we are oftentimes fighting against ourselves. Where remembrance is like a telescope, keeping the future in mind, concentration is a microscope focusing on the present, which is right in front of you. It means constantly staring at the moment, knowing it is the brick being used to build the dream that you will dwell in later. Your

P.R.O.C.E.S.S

success and dream demand that you stay committed and know that you can't expect your goals to be reached by wishful thinking, but by methodical effort.

Encouragement

You are going to have to be an encouragement to yourself every single step of the way. If you are able to, surround yourself with encouragers who urge you on when you want to give up. Encouragement is an act of courage within oneself; it's "In-Couragement." It should be a turbine that is continuously spinning, giving you the energy to keep going. It needs to be a generator that runs even if the power is down around you due to the hurricanes that life brings your way. The word of God is full of promises and reminders of power, strength, and authority. We can and should find encouragement, knowing that God is walking with us every step. Having courage is not to say that anxiety and hesitation don't exist, but it is making an effort to act in spite of it.

Supplication

Philippians 4:6 New King James Version (NKJV)
"Be anxious for nothing, but in everything by prayer and supplication, with thanksgiving, let your requests be made known to God;"

Supplication is a powerful word that carries a deep meaning. It speaks to the importance of petition and bringing needs over to the Lord. We serve an amazing God who desires to walk with us in the hardest moments. While we are walking through our valleys or standing on our mountaintops, God sees us and is waiting to stretch out His able hands to help. The role of the Holy Spirit in the life of a believer is a powerful aspect that empowers, equips, and transforms.

131

Never overlook the importance of prayer and worship while you are contending for your dream or breakthrough. I am a father, and I can tell you that I would do anything to see my son succeed and prosper. I love him with every ounce within me, and to think that is how our Heavenly Father loves us is humbling. He is not just a God sitting on a throne but the Father who is cheering you on. Don't stay silent on your journey, but talk to Jesus in prayer and make sure you open the text message of the Word of God.

Strength

David found the importance of this truth in a time in his life when he needed it the most. It is hard being strong all the time, and we all will encounter times of weaknesses. We need to ensure that in the hard times when it seems like nothing is working out, and everyone wants to turn against us, that we stay strong.

1 Samuel 30:1-8
30 *David and his men reached Ziklag on the third day. Now the Amalekites had raided the Negev and Ziklag. They had attacked Ziklag and burned it, ² and had taken captive the women and everyone else in it, both young and old. They killed none of them, but carried them off as they went on their way. ³ When David and his men reached Ziklag, they found it destroyed by fire and their wives and sons and daughters taken captive. ⁴ So David and his men wept aloud until they had no strength left to weep. ⁵ David's two wives had been captured—Ahinoam of Jezreel and Abigail, the widow of Nabal of Carmel. ⁶ David was greatly distressed because the men were talking of stoning him; each one was bitter in spirit because of his sons and daughters. But David found strength in the Lord his God. ⁷ Then David said to Abiathar the priest, the son of Ahimelek, "Bring me the ephod." Abiathar brought it to*

him, [8] and David inquired of the Lord, "Shall I pursue this raiding party? Will I overtake them?" "Pursue them," he answered. "You will certainly overtake them and succeed in the rescue."

It is remarkable that David found strength in the Lord. When the same brothers who fought alongside him were going to betray him and stone him, he paused and encouraged himself. When you are fighting uphill towards your dreams, you must know that it is war. It is a war with your mind that is demanding you to quit, but draw a line in the sand and refuse to be bullied. Life is like a weight room. We will have weight on top of us that we feel like we can't budge. But I am thankful that Jesus is our spotter, helping us lift it, yet at the same time not always lifting it for us. It's like a two-finger spot, and it's just enough to aid you with the rep but not too much such that you didn't do any lifting. After all, it is the process in the iron jungle that will make you stronger. A challenging exercise in the gym is when you are doing negative workouts. Take the bench press for example, the spotter helps you get the weight off the rack, but you have to lower the weight down slowly. It is the eccentric rep that is making you stronger by holding on as long as you can. When the bar gets down to your chest, the spotter grabs the barbell and lifts it back to the top of the rep, only for you to do it again. It is an exercise that uses negativity to make you stronger. We must learn how to be strong during the brightest times of positivity in our lives because we have worked out in the most negative conditions. It is the repetitions in the gym of life that make us stronger. So one day, the things, mindsets, tasks or problems that used to weigh us down are only our warm-up. It's not a big deal because we have endured the process and become stronger because of it.

You are an overcomer, and by the grace of God you will step over every mountain and conquer every trial that comes your way. Don't allow frustration to throw you into the locker and give you a wedgie.

Stop being intimidated every time frustration tries to bully you and push you around. You have been going to the gym and are stronger than ever. Show that bully that you aren't a pushover. Charge after that education, put that business in a headlock, stand up for your dreams. Listen closely. Can you hear his belittling words trying to break you down again? Well, this is your chance!

CHAPTER 9:
SUCCESS AND REGRETS

Toy Cars

I have an amazing son named Hezekiah, and like many toddlers, he enjoys playing with toys. The moment I get home and I place my bag down in my office, he grabs me by the hand to go into his room to play. He owns a bunch of cars and loves playing with them by sending them down a slide to crash into blocks.

"Daddy do you want to race?" he asks as he grabs his favorite toy car while handing me one, and we head to the hallway.

So there we are like the start of a NASCAR race, making the revving sound of our engines with our mouths, echoing off the walls. Ready, set, go! But before we can see the cars launch forward, we have to pull the cars back until we hear clicks and feel resistance.

Like many times spending time with my family, I witness another valuable life lesson: sometimes you have to be pulled back before you can be launched forward. Taking steps back to reassess your life is an essential habit of reflection that we should often do. I hope that by this point in the book you have had the hard and challenging conversations with yourself that you may have been

> sometimes you have to be pulled back before you can be launched forward.

putting off for a while. Maybe you realized that you have been lazy, doubtful, and fearful. When you pulled back the layers, perhaps you discovered insecurity was driving the car of your life all along. You made up in your mind that you aren't going to waste any more time but seize the moment, knowing that this is your chance. The time to start moving more aggressively towards your purpose is right now.

The alarm just went off, and it is time to clock into work at the office of your life. There needs to be a healthy evaluation of your actions, past, habits, personality, and trends so you can drive through the walls that are in your way. But in order to change what needs to be improved, we need to be able to pinpoint the challenges. Whether you are stepping into a new year or just stepping into the next day, we are the common denominator that is consistent in every situation. If we desire the future to be successful and to put a restraining order against our regrets, it will take intentional effort. In order to reach your goals, a plan must be put in place. Yet, even before that, we need to do a deep dive into who we are that may have aided the issues to arise or continue, but also bring the success to come and stay.

Inventory

In some facet or another, we all have areas of success and areas of regrets. Things that, when we look back in our past, we did right and matters that need improvement. If we would dare to go even further, we will discover there has been a cycle of the regrets for months or even years. It is imperative as you step to the starting line, be prepared to race toward your dreams, goals, and aspirations, that you know what it will take to win. Just as important is taking inventory of your life to discover the reasons why you have been losing. Every new year, many people around the world make New Year's resolutions, but few stick to them and even fewer map out a plan on how to achieve them.

Realism and pessimism are not the same things. Pessimism is a rational way one may have to see life and its issues with a "glass is half full" viewpoint. Pessimists may see what they don't have before they acknowledge what they do have in life. Whereas a realist simply acknowledges that the glass has water in it. It is a starting point, and "it is what it is." As you take the deep dive into your past, this isn't the moment to invite condemnation into your house and be consumed by its degrading words. Nor is it a time to call pride and listen to its sweet words to blow up your ego. Sometimes we need to be like a rubber band; we need to be pulled back before we can be launched forward.

Make a List

Make a list. On one side write or type **success**, and on the other side write **regrets**. Starting off with the success column first, write out areas that you believe went very well last year. Areas that you have conquered, seen growth, and other positive affairs. What were mountains that you climbed over this past year that you have been aspiring to defeat for a while? Keep in mind that not all areas of success are connected to a dollar sign. Money in and of itself is not a telltale sign that something is successful. Maybe some areas of success or achievement that happened were that you went to college, trade school, or learned a skill. Perhaps you got married, lost weight, started a business, or reconciled a relationship. Maybe you got hired into your dream job or a job a step closer to your dream job.

After you write out areas that you were successful in, it is time to write out areas of regret. What are the areas that you are still trying to make happen? Maybe you didn't drop the fifty pounds or start college like you said you were going to. Maybe you didn't save money or invest it as you had planned. Maybe you were in a horrible relationship that cost you so much time, pain, and money.

Now that you have written out the successes and regrets, it is time for soul searching even deeper, because you must ask yourself why. Why did these things become successful this year, and why do you have these regrets? The goal is to continue to succeed, yet end the regrets, but this will only happen when you break the cycle by discovering what is spinning the wheel.

Success

I can't stress enough how this honesty exercise can transform your life and make you a better person in many aspects. You can become a better parent, boss, spouse or employee because you are taking the voyage to destination "why." I will never forget when I did this for myself; it changed my life, perspective, and viewpoint about my future. Success is my and your own responsibility, and we must take it by the reins and steer it. I created my list towards the end of 2015, and to say that the year was challenging would be the understatement of the year. I told myself that I had a year to work as hard as I could without any excuses. I held myself accountable, and I was amazed at the results. I did this each year and wanted to get better and build a legacy for my family.

The first thing I wrote down in my life was my family. My family is my first ministry, and I stand by that with everything within me. My son was born in 2016, and in 2017, my wife and I took our first real vacation since we have been married. That was a massive win for me because our livelihood was a complete faith walk at times. The reason why it was a success for us was that we lived in moments that we knew there was no way we could afford to go on a memorable vacation.

I wrote down my first book, **_Crowns Are Greater Than Trophies_**, as a place of success for countless reasons. For one, it was a testament to myself that I wasn't dumb, and I was no longer living underneath that slavery mindset. Secondly, the book was and is a massive blessing to a bunch of people all around the nation as marriages and families are being healed. People are starting to break generational bondages, chains, and behaviors, and are fighting for each other rather than fighting each other. Take a deep dive in your life and take a moment to celebrate it. Listen, in a day and time where people are tearing each other apart, you must take moments to encourage yourself. What are some areas of success in your life, and why were they successful?

Knowing is half the battle, because now you must track down the reasoning behind your success so you can continue it. Maybe the reason why you got promoted at work was because you were the hardest worker in the room. You showed up on time and you left when the task was finished. You worked in a spirit of excellence that separated you from the rest of the employees. Maybe the reason why you were able to get out of debt was that you saved your money and cooked more often at home. The "why" is just as important and possibly more critical as sole acknowledgment in and of itself.

Regrets

Letdowns and failures happen to all of us, it is part of life. We can make a choice to learn from them or to make those moments our own death bed. Regrets are issues that you may wish you handled differently or simply handled at all. Nothing is fixed with time, and problems rarely go away. The only thing that goes away with time is the chance to fix them. You have a moment in your life to turn things around, break toxic cycles, and face that bully of your purpose head-on. As I have shared in this book many times, I was a prisoner of my own regrets, yet came to adopt them as the normalcy of my life. One of the regrets I had that I know I failed at drastically was the utilization of my time. The kick that I needed, which truly opened my eyes, was an email from an unexpected place. I saved the screenshot on my phone, and I have it to this day as a testament and reminder to keep turning things around. That unexpected source was an email I received from Xbox.

I love playing video games as a tool to unwind, relax, and rest. When I was finished with work or back home from traveling on the road, I would play Xbox live late at night until sometimes early in the morning. I would completely lose track of time, yet still had to get up early the next day. I want to be very clear that there is nothing wrong whatsoever with playing or owning an Xbox or video game system. However, my time management was horrendous and needed a wakeup call.

Towards the end of every year, Xbox sends an email that gives you different stats about your game placement, experience, and standing around the world. It was at the end of the year 2015, and here is what the year-end review stated. "In 2015 you spent 2510 hours gaming on Xbox live." There are only 8760 hours in an entire year. Then it compared me with my friend's gaming and said that "on average your friends spent 937 hours gaming on Xbox live." This next part was the needle that broke the camel's back for me: it stated that "Your gaming house places you in the top 5% of all Xbox players worldwide." I remember as if it was yesterday, staring at my phone in amazement. I was immediately challenged to not only play less videogames, but to use my time more wisely.

Time Management

But just as before, simply knowing the issue is not going to keep it from happening again. We need to ask ourselves why. Why was

I on Xbox for so long and what could I do to change it? I didn't want to completely stop playing video games, as it was an excellent way for me to relax and also a chance to connect with friends and family around the nation. But I knew that my why was that I didn't think I could study, read or use that time for anything else because I didn't think I could do anything else. When I realized that I wasn't dumb, but more than capable of bettering myself, I chose to give more attention to my time. I had to learn to say no to myself and no to others. I went to college, and I used the time that I used to play games for studying or learning. I discovered that I had no problem completing the task that was given to me in the office. I now know that it was because I had more vision for others' goals than for my own.

At the beginning of my turnaround season, I took some drastic steps to help me manage my time and complete tasks more efficiently. I went to Walmart, purchased a kitchen timer, and put it on my desk for fifteen-minute increments, and started my reading journey there. I rearranged my cellphone and put all my productivity apps on the front and the social media and time-draining apps in the far back of my phone, in a folder, so it took more effort to reach it.

A huge gamechanger for me was that I learned how to study myself. I had to look within myself and discover when I was the most alert, creative, and could pay attention to details. I learned what I can and cannot eat that affects my productivity. I rearranged how I completed my tasks and did the detailed and tedious assignments in the morning before lunch. After lunch, I did my meetings and brainstorming sessions. I learned that my creativity comes and goes and that I had to jump on the train when it was passing by. The single factor of taking control of my time turned so many things around for me. If your time is running away from you, I believe that once you get it under control, it can turn things around for you.

Relationships

But maybe one of your regrets doesn't look like mine. We are all different and have different temperaments and personalities. Could yours be not starting your business, or not spending more time with your family, or bad relationships? You can always tell when someone just broke up on social media because the "All men are dogs" posts or the "ladies are gold-diggers" messages start to appear. Maybe you look in your past, and it seems like you don't have any luck with relationships. Remember to ask yourself the brave question: why? Before you start pointing fingers at the other person, make sure you are pointing them at yourself first. Take some portion of the responsibility pie. After all, you decided to get in a relationship with them. Maybe they were unfaithful, lied all the time, or weren't trustworthy. Those, along with many other reasons, are indeed grounds to end a relationship. But the why behind the regrets must go deeper than that. Why did you pick him or her? What state of life were you in when you got in the relationship? Were you lonely or desperate? Were you just so attracted by their physical appearance that you overlooked their personality?

Taking things even more in-depth as you go through your history browser, how often have you found yourself in heartbreak? Do you find yourself getting into a relationship with the same kind of girl or guy, with the same character flaws but with different faces? If you do, then the brave and hard thing to do is to make sure you add yourself as part of the problem, so you can solve the relational equation in your life. Why do you keep picking those kinds of people to hook up with and give your heart to? Why are you getting into a relationship with someone who doesn't share your same morals or convictions? Did you just want someone to say "I love you" because you didn't hear it often growing up? Do you find yourself going to the same kind of toxic environments to find a spouse and are surprised why things aren't working out? It is vital to address the why within us so we can break the cycles and turn those regrets to success.

Money

Maybe you regret that you didn't make or save more money. You filed your taxes and were amazed at how much money you made, but you have no idea where all the money went. Remember to ask why and follow the breadcrumbs to see where the hole may be located. As soon as you finish this chapter, go online and print out your bank statement for the year. Grab a highlighter and highlight every time you ate out, and also every time you got a snack at a gas station or a convenience store. Highlight your trips to your favorite coffee spots or bars. If you're playing the lottery, highlight the times, you purchased a lottery ticket or how much money you spend on toxic, addictive behaviors such as cigarettes or cigars.

Make sure you are sitting down when you do this, because it may be shocking when you see the results. Our stomachs are bottomless pits and our taste buds seem as if they lead us far before our brains do. Let's say that every day in the mornings you stop by your favorite coffee shop on the way to work and spend $5. You work Monday through Friday, so this comes to twenty days a month, if we just round up to four weeks in a month. With that alone, you would have spent $25 a week for four weeks in a month, which comes to $100. Thus, in a year you spent $1,200 on a coffee that may have tasted amazing, but you completely forgot about it ten seconds after the last sip. The $1,200 that you spent on your morning coffee would be more than enough money for you to start your LLC and your eCommerce business. I am not suggesting for a second that you can't or shouldn't treat yourself to a good cup of coffee every now and then, but if money is the issue, stop looking at it as "it's just $5."

The problem may have never been that you didn't make enough money this year. Maybe it was the fact that you didn't steward it wisely. Or maybe you see that you need to make more money, so you know you need to get another job or find another way to add more income. But to look at your life and highlight the fact that you are broke isn't going to break the cycle but keep it going.

Backdoor Passes

I remember playing basketball in high school. One day, the coach brought a more experienced and mature team to scrimmage against us. At first, I was thinking, "What in the world is the coach thinking? He must know we are going to lose." Sure enough, we got stomped, and the score was embarrassing. I can still recall the lesson the coach was trying to give us that day, and he highlighted the reason why we lost. The team we played against didn't shoot a bunch of threes or do highlight-reel dunks. They racked up points using a simple and fundamental basketball move called a backdoor pass and used picks and rolls. The coach always preached to see the ball and the man at all times. He practiced pistol set positions in practice seemingly every day, but when it was time to execute what we learned, we missed the mark. The opposing team just used picks and rolls and backdoor passes. They would set a screen and wait for us to get blocked even for a second and pass the ball. Over and over the coach would yell out that we had to communicate. We had to be a team and call the picks and screens when they were happening, or tell another player to pick up a different man on defense. Our entire team was broken down by simple, foundational, and fundamental basketball moves.

Are you constantly scratching your head, wondering why you feel like you are losing in the game called life? Are you wondering why you keep getting beat year after year with the same issues? It may be the little things that you don't see when you take your eyes off the ball, prize, and goal. This is your moment to reassess your year and get back in the game. Find coaches, mentors, or courses that will give you the experience to succeed as you start communicating your needs. Celebrate your moments of success and confront your times of regret, but make sure you ask yourself "why" and break the cycle. You are called to win, and you are destined to win. I hear your legacy in the crowd calling out your name. It is game time, put on your jersey, and lace up your sneakers. The coach just called you in, this is your shot, and this is your chance!

CHAPTER 10
LOTTERY TICKET

———•◆•———

Towards the last few weeks of every year, churches around the world make different declarations. I do not believe there is anything inherently wrong with this at all; however, if we don't have a grasp of the full picture, we can mislead ourselves. Pastors make declarations like this: "2008: the year of blessings," or "2019: the year of breakthrough." To be very clear, I don't believe this is wrong, and the declaration is important.

In my church, Trinity Church, the pastors placed banners in the sanctuary stating "Freedom." They have been praying for freedom over the lives of the people and also over the church. It is extremely fitting because a few months into 2019 they announced that the church was debt-free.

The church campus is amazing, with a large sanctuary, an amazing school teaching from preschool all the way to high school. But through the years the church was in $3.2 million in debt from building projects and many other things that were way before my day. When my pastors, Jamie and Michelle Jones took over as lead pastors, he declared to the church that we would be out of debt by the year 2020. I am sure that some people may have thought, "How in the world would this happen?" But they went on an aggressive mission, snowballing the debt, and took the debt that was accumulated from the years of ministry and paid it in full. I was there in the Debt Freedom Celebration Service, and it was amazing.

To add to how incredible this was, people decided to not only support that cause but to examine their own lives. They got serious about confronting areas where they needed freedom. The testimonies of people getting blessed or becoming debt-free themselves were too much to count. The point that we must see in this story is that they had to get involved in their own deliverance aggressively. When Pastor Jamie declared that we would be debt-free, the church just didn't start praying about it and leaving it there. No, they worked hard towards the goal. They sacrificed and grinded hard to finally be standing in the place they are today. Like many things God is trying to put into our hands, it requires action, commitment, dedication, and of course, His powerful grace. Stop leaving your success up to the roll of the dice. No longer gamble with your future, hoping something will be different.

Scratch-off tickets

As Christians, we use the word "favor" very loosely, and I also believe not in the complete context in which it should be used or expected. We pray that God gives us favor as if it is a scratch-off lottery ticket, hoping that we win. We treat it as some mystical spell that God puts on some people and delegates to others. I firmly believe that God can and will touch your life, and that is an amazing experience to be in. But when we start to live expecting a discount, raise or promotion without working, preparing, and even being qualified for it, then we need to rethink what favor really is. Once again, I am not suggesting that God doesn't pour out blessings just because He wants to, because that would be far from the truth. We serve a Father who desires to shower His children with blessings during His time. That is His grace at work. But it is the waiting in the middle between blessings and hardship that we may be over-looking. It is the misuse of our time in between the random blessings that won't prepare us to live blessed.

Favor is the physical embodiment of grace, and grace is the spiritual embodiment of love. Favor happens **to** you, but grace happens **in** you. However, favor is both received and prepared for.

Favor is the physical embodiment of grace, and grace is the spiritual embodiment of love. Favor happens to you, but grace happens in you.

Positioned for Favor

Proverbs 3
Wisdom Bestows Well-Being

3 My son, do not forget my teaching,
but keep my commands in your heart,
2 for they will prolong your life many years
and bring you peace and prosperity.
3 Let love and faithfulness never leave you;
bind them around your neck,
write them on the tablet of your heart.
4 Then you will win favor and a good name
in the sight of God and man.
5 Trust in the Lord with all your heart
and lean not on your own understanding;
6 in all your ways submit to him,
and he will make your paths straight.
7 Do not be wise in your own eyes;
fear the Lord and shun evil.

⁸ *This will bring health to your body*
and nourishment to your bones.
⁹ *Honor the Lord with your wealth,*
with the firstfruits of all your crops;
¹⁰ *then your barns will be filled to overflowing,*
and your vats will brim over with new wine.
¹¹ *My son, do not despise the Lord's discipline,*
and do not resent his rebuke,
¹² *because the Lord disciplines those he loves,*
as a father the son he delights in.
¹³ *Blessed are those who find wisdom,*
those who gain understanding,
¹⁴ *for she is more profitable than silver*
and yields better returns than gold.
¹⁵ *She is more precious than rubies;*
nothing you desire can compare with her.
¹⁶ *Long life is in her right hand;*
in her left hand are riches and honor.
¹⁷ *Her ways are pleasant ways,*
and all her paths are peace.
¹⁸ *She is a tree of life to those who take hold of her;*
those who hold her fast will be blessed.
¹⁹ *By wisdom the Lord laid the earth's foundations,*
by understanding he set the heavens in place;
²⁰ *by his knowledge the watery depths were divided,*
and the clouds let drop the dew.
²¹ *My son, do not let wisdom and understanding out of*
your sight,
preserve sound judgment and discretion;
²² *they will be life for you,*
an ornament to grace your neck.
²³ *Then you will go on your way in safety,*

and your foot will not stumble.
²⁴ When you lie down, you will not be afraid;
when you lie down, your sleep will be sweet.
²⁵ Have no fear of sudden disaster
or of the ruin that overtakes the wicked,
²⁶ for the Lord will be at your side
and will keep your foot from being snared.
²⁷ Do not withhold good from those to whom it is due,
when it is in your power to act.
²⁸ Do not say to your neighbor,
"Come back tomorrow and I'll give it to you"—
when you already have it with you.
²⁹ Do not plot harm against your neighbor,
who lives trustfully near you.
³⁰ Do not accuse anyone for no reason—
when they have done you no harm.
³¹ Do not envy the violent
or choose any of their ways.
³² For the Lord detests the perverse
but takes the upright into his confidence.
³³ The Lord's curse is on the house of the wicked,
but he blesses the home of the righteous.
³⁴ He mocks proud mockers
but shows favor to the humble and oppressed.
³⁵ The wise inherit honor,
but fools get only shame.

The book of Proverbs is a powerful and transparent book of the Bible that is full of wisdom for us to live out to the best of our abilities. I love this passage of scripture because it lays out a plan to be blessed. They are verses that are connected to both a cause and an effect. They aren't random things God may do, but byproducts of doing what needs to be done. An effort is involved in positioning yourself for favor and blessings. Having a strong work ethic and being well mannered can get you very far in life. If you are serious enough to seize your chance, read the passage carefully. Excuses are the red tape that laziness uses to keep your dreams at bay as it stares at your potential from a distance.

> Excuses are the red tape that laziness uses to keep your dreams at bay as it stares at your potential from a distance.

Verses 1 and 2 give us a reminder to not to forget the teaching on wisdom but to retain the information and apply it. If we do, we can expect to yield a harvest of peace and prosperity. Keeping God's commands and the wisdom that is connected to it in our hearts is important. The Bible tells us that our hearts are the wellspring of our lives. Just like our physical heart pumps blood to our entire body, so does our spiritual heart. Whatever state the heart is in, whether good or bad, will affect other issues of the body. If unforgiveness is in your heart, it is going to pump that into your mind so you withhold your love for a person, or maybe to your lips as you share toxic words. If lust is in your heart, it is going to pump that into your eyes and hands so you will look at things that are ungodly, and touch or click on things or people that you shouldn't. In the same manner, if we have compassion in our hearts, it is going to pump to our hands as we give the hungry person some food. It is going to pump it to our mouths as we encourage the person who is feeling down and depressed. Notice that the verse doesn't say to put it simply in our minds, but our hearts. It is not in the arena that war is waged within us, or could just be a mental assent or agreement. Rather when it is in your heart, it affects your entire life.

Verses 3 and 4 are a command to let love and faithfulness never leave us, and speak to consistently and continually. Faithfulness is a vital aspect to understand because it is directly connected to verse

4 and the good fortune that is ahead. The result of faithfulness and love always being present in everything that we do is that we will gain favor and a good name with both God and man. I hope you caught what Solomon was saying in verses 3 and 4, because this may directly be connected to your current state of life and also how you can better your life. The promise is that we will win favor in the eyes of God and man. How do you win favor in the eyes of God? Obedience to His word and living your life for Him are just a few ways, and we can't discount how God just blesses us just to bless us.

The second part is where I believe many Christians today miss out, learning how to turn this around and turn your life around. The Bible says, "you will win favor and a GOOD NAME in the sight of God and man." I believe your favor in the sight of man is directly connected to the good name you have made for yourself due to your faithfulness and consistency. This may step on some toes and maybe even hurt, but please know that I am not trying to be a bounty hunter, but a nurse preparing you to meet with the Great Physician. Maybe you aren't experiencing the level of favor that you could be because your work ethic is not very good. Do you show up to work late and leave early? Is your performance under par, or do you do your job to the best of your ability? Do you make social media posts like you hate your job and complain about going in? Are you not a team player and have a horrible attitude at work? Are you reliable and trustworthy, and when you say you are going to do something, do you do it?

How can you expect favor via a promotion with better pay and more responsibility when you are not a great steward with what you are over now? Don't make an excuse and say, "Well, the Lord knows my heart." That may be the case, but your boss needs to see your actions. Have we become so lazy in our walk with the Lord that we are expecting the Lord to move us to higher levels without us putting in our work and being faithful? Favor can be prepared for, and I firmly believe it is presented on the road of hard work. Ask yourself these hard questions, be completely honest and transparent: Would you hire you? Would you want to promote you? It's not always if a person feels they deserve it, but have they earned it.

Do you have a good work ethic or are you saying you will get it done later? Procrastination places faith in an unknown and unguaranteed chance such as "tomorrow," while trading the opportunity to act and do what needs to be done today. Your time is a seed, and your actions in the fields of potential are the sowing process. If you don't plant, use or occupy your time wisely today, then tomorrow you will be standing in the same field of wishful thinking. Laziness, blaming others, and a demanding sense of entitlement are oftentimes the byproduct of an individual who has wasted his time. So the question that all of us need to bring to our attention every day is: How am I going to use my time at work wisely?

What have you been telling yourself to give yourself permission to be lazy? As stated in a previous chapter, there is a MASSIVE difference between rest and laziness. Resting is a time of reprieve after productive work has been done. But laziness is the awareness of a task, goal, or assignment, yet choosing to ignore the need. Laziness does the minimum required to get by and get it done(ish). Laziness is not putting your cart back at the store. Laziness is changing your mind about an item at checkout, yet refusing to get out of line to place the item in the proper place. Laziness views inconvenience as impossibilities rather than obstacles. Laziness elevates the need to the wielder of the deceptive mindset over others, stating internally, "It's their job." How many tasks has God given to us that we have ignored, derailed, or missed because of laziness? While at the same time praying to God in our Sunday morning services, asking the Lord for favor at work.

All throughout the chapter, you can read promise after promise that are always connected to cause and effect. It's a promise that if you do this, God will do that. We can see this pattern of actions throughout the entire Bible. If you are going to seize your chance, then you must have a strong work ethic. Choose to become the hardest working person in the room and make a future for yourself. Even the word of God speaks of the work ethic that Christians should have.

Colossians 3:23
"Whatever you do, work at it with all your heart, as working for the Lord, not for human masters,"

My father's life lesson

My father was a very hard worker and had a hustle and grind that it seemed few could keep up with. At the time of this writing, my dad has suffered three strokes that turned his life upside down. It affected his memory, motor functions, and other issues. I remember driving up from Florida to see him shortly after his strokes, he had no idea who I was. It was very disheartening to say the least, but my family chose to keep believing and praying. He has been getting progressively better, we celebrate that every day.

But I remember the first thought I had when I saw him after his strokes. He had a cold stare past me and once again had no idea who I was. I remember like it was yesterday. I told myself that I was so glad that I told him thank you. I would tell him thank you repeatedly and send him encouraging text messages during one of the hardest seasons of his and my family's lives. I would remind him that he was made for greatness and thank him for showing us a strong work ethic. There isn't such a thing as perfect parents because there isn't such a thing as a perfect person. I made a choice to try my best to focus on what went right and celebrate that.

My dad traveled in a band and played many instruments as well as sang amazingly well. He also worked in factories and did odd jobs around the community to make extra money. He would oftentimes take us along to cut people's grass, rake leaves or weed around lakes and ponds. Looking back, I celebrate that my dad had a lawn care business; yes, without the flash and glamor, but a business nonetheless. My dad, Kenneth McCain would build dog houses and sell them around the city also, so he was in sales. He was an entrepreneur in his own right and had a level of ingenuity to fix things with random items. My dad was the first person to help someone when they were down, and though he didn't have money, would lend a helping hand. He could stretch a dollar farther than anyone I have ever seen, so he lived out economics.

His wall wasn't covered with degrees, but he learned from the school of hard knocks. My dad would quote a phrase often to us and himself, "It is how you count your blessings." He taught us how to give a solid handshake and a proper "yes sir" and "no sir." These characteristics that were instilled in me, I believe, are the reason why I have received so many promotions in my life. I have been elevated to positions that I wondered how I got there, and I was thriving in that element. Without a shadow of a doubt, I know the favor I gained in the eyes of man comes from being the hardest worker in the room can be traced down to all the times I was forced to go work with my dad. The conversations around the yard, raking the mountains of leaves in the North Carolina fall breeze, became deposits of seeds in my life that would bring an amazing harvest.

Your credit score

This is your chance to turn things around and shift your reputation in your workplace, if needed. This is your chance to wake up on time, to start moving towards your dreams, plans, and goals. This is your chance to study harder, work more efficiently, and position yourself for a level of favor that can change your life. Your credit score is an indication of your loan worthiness as if you have a record of paying on time, among other things. It is an indication to the banks if they can trust you at your word via the application you filled out. If your score is poor or bad, you have a hard chance of getting a loan or make a purchase without insane rates. However, if your score is good or excellent, banks and good credit card companies will be happy to work with you because you have a history of trustworthiness. Don't walk through life with your work ethic scoring low and expect opportunities to be handed to you. If you don't make your payments or due dates at work, or have been delinquent and been written up by collections or the human resources office due to bad behavior, you aren't positioning yourself for favor.

It is time that you turn your credit history around. Show the relationships around you that you have a level of trustworthiness to be respected. Work smarter and work harder, because when favor knocks on your door, you better be ready to walk through it. Stop leaving your future up to chance and spending your paycheck on lottery tickets, hoping that this is your big break. Get a good night's rest, wake up, and eat a balanced breakfast, because this is your chance.

CHAPTER 11
TAKE A KNEE

One of my favorite films to watch is a movie called *After Earth*, directed by M. Night Shyamalan. It stars one of my favorite actors, Will Smith, and his son, Jaden. It is a science fiction movie that involves them crash landing on a hostile Earth a thousand years into the future. Things are overgrown, dangerous, and intense, and the son finds himself traversing through the land physically alone. Will Smith played the role of General Cypher Raige, a high-ranking officer respected by many for his ability to kill Ursa's, these were horrifying creatures that were blind but could smell fear. Jaden played the role of a cadet and son of the general named Kitai, tasked with shooting a beacon to get help. However, the beacon was in the other half of the broken ship. To add to the magnitude of the situation General Cypher is severely wounded in the crash and cannot go with his son to retrieve the beacon, and it is a task that only Kitai can do if they both want to survive. But even though father is not physically with son, they are able to talk to each other.

To make matters worse, one of the Ursa's, one that killed without hesitation and tracked its prey by smelling fear, broke out due to the crash and is on the loose. This is a fear that has been in the center of the general's life, because an Ursa killed his own sister years ago. I don't want to ruin the movie for you, so I won't give any spoilers. This movie is a must-watch, and many aspects of the film spoke to me.

Maybe you have felt that you have crashed landed into a season in your life where you have been tasked with responsibility that placed not only your life, but your family's lives in your hands. Maybe you know what it is like to feel the fear of the unknown, yet you know if you don't fight forward, nothing will change. Kitai and General Cypher had to take their chances and so do you. Here are a few lessons that I learned in the movie that truly apply to our lives today.

A Guiding Voice

Even though Kitai was tasked to get the beacon alone, he had his father's voice guiding him along the way. I love how the Lord is always walking with us in the good times and the bad. We are never alone, forgotten, or overlooked in even the most trying times in our lives. I believe one of the reasons many don't take the leap into the unknown is a fear of abandonment and isolation, but the Lord is with us. When we look into the future, a lot of unknown circumstances can cause some to persuade themselves never to step out of the ship. We can think of all the dangers the future may have in store and shackle ourselves in uncertainty. The Word of God tells us that God is the pioneer of our faith. A pioneer is a person who goes into uncharted territories and can map out the place; thus, when returning, they are able to lead others into new lands. We can have confidence that when we look into our future, even though there are things that are unknown to us, He is very aware of them. Trust the voice of the Holy Spirit as you take your chance. Read the text message of the Word of God and gain wisdom, understanding, and direction. Trust God when some doors are shut and others feel like they are slow to open. Understand that rejection in life can

sometimes be one of the greatest gifts God can give you, because
He has your future in mind. Think about your life right now, how
many of the prayer requests that you used to pray weren't answered,
and now you thank God for it.

Have you thanked Him for the relationship, which wasn't
even in God's will for your life, that didn't work out? Now you are
holding the hand of your bride and staring your legacy in the eyes
as they hug you and call you mommy or daddy. Have you thanked
Him for all the times you didn't get hired so, like in chess, you were
positioned for the job you have now that has better pay and better
hours? It is hard to praise God in the midst of rejection, but when
we view it as redirection and steering of our attention, it is easy to
understand. The fear of abandonment is a real thing and has been a
self-inflicted wound for so many. The sobering fact is that the road
of success towards your dreams and goals isn't always paved, as it is
a road less traveled. It doesn't have a lot of traffic, and it is not easy
to get to, but you are going to make it. So don't fret, because your
heavenly Father is your tour guide in the excursion of life.

Isaiah 43:2
When you pass through the waters,
I will be with you;
and when you pass through the rivers,
they will not sweep over you.
When you walk through the fire,
you will not be burned;
the flames will not set you ablaze.

In addition to the voice of God that we have to lead and guide
us, we also have the people around us. There are wise and experienced people around the world who may have been where you are
going. It is important to try to find healthy, proven, and trusted

voices to learn and glean from, in both their successes and failures. Reading is also a great way to gain wisdom and knowledge so you can become even more equipped as you take the journey. Books are a great and oftentimes overlooked recourse that many people don't appreciate. But when we read, we can glean decades of a person's life experiences from a single book. Seek out knowledge and trusted voices that have your best interest in mind, as they may be a gamechanger for you. They can help you ask the right questions, give tips for giving a business proposal, share relationship advice, and this list can go on and on. The "lone wolf persona" that may seem cool on Instagram may not be useful in real life.

Proverbs 15:22
"Plans fail for lack of counsel, but with many advisers, they succeed."

Fear Triggers

The Ursa is blind and cannot track its prey in any way other than smelling people's fear. When it is hunting and on the prowl, it sets up traps to invoke the fear pheromone to excrete, like a shark that smells blood in the ocean. The traps are graphic, and Kitai comes across one while on the mission given to him by his father. To tell you more than this would spoil the movie, so you need to watch it and find out.

This is such an accurate representation of life, because you will discover moments in your future that could trigger fear and the desire to quit. The fight or flight response is authentic, and it's a tug of war that everyone combats in some way or another. Fear triggers are things like needing capital, but you don't know how you are going to save it up. Maybe you get a bad report from the doctor, in that moment you sense an overwhelming fear of the unknown. You and your spouse hit a hard time in y'all's relationship, and it is at a breaking point. The arguments and repeated disagreements bring the fear that y'all may divorce to a boiling point. Perhaps you are about to transition full-time into your business instead of working for someone else. There are many examples of fear triggers in our lives, but we must overcome them and keep pressing forward. The General went through a moment where he faced fear and mastered it. While telling his son about his experience with the Ursa, he gave every viewer powerful words of wisdom.

"Fear is not real. The only place that fear can exist is in our thoughts of the future. It is a product of our imagination, causing us to fear things that do not at present and may not ever exist. That is near insanity, Kitai. Now, do not misunderstand me. Danger is very real. But fear is a choice. We are all telling ourselves a story. And that day mine changed."

Wow! "Danger is very real. But fear is a choice." As you are lacing up your sneakers, about to step on the starting line to run to your purpose, keep that truth in your mind. The fear triggers will appear all throughout your race, but for you and your legacy's sake, don't stop running. As you commit to becoming the doctor, the road will be challenging. When you want to quit because of the workload and the sacrifice you made to give up a social life for a season, it will be worth it. You will know that it was worth it all, not when you get handed a diploma or walk across the stage, which are just amazing honors, but you will know that it is worth it when you save the life of a dying person or help patients get well. When they tell you, "Thank you," and you see them rise up from the bed of their affliction, you will know that it was worth fighting forward.

Two of the scariest moments of my life were when I became a husband, and later became a father. I had a lot of questions, and I didn't want to make any mistakes. Before I proposed to my wife, I was hesitant about asking her to be my wife because I wanted to have everything perfect. I didn't want her stepping into anything unstable, as I desired to break a cycle that can be traced down throughout my generational history. I had a house, a car and a great job with steady pay and benefits, but I kept excusing myself, chasing after the rabbit in front of me. I was scared to take the leap. I went out with a friend named Zac to Buffalo Wild Wings, and he challenged my thinking. I was using my past pain as fear triggers in my life as an excuse not to take the leap. It was a conversation that changed my life. *After Earth* is a movie that I can say without a doubt is one of the many aids that have helped me confront the fears within myself. God can use anything to reach us, and for me, it was this movie.

Take a Knee

Another intense scene that screamed to me during the movie was how they managed anxiety, uncertainty, and many other dynamics by taking a knee. The boy tasked to get the beacon was only out in the wilderness for a short period of time before he confronted his first obstacle. He heard loud noises and was not sure what it was, the General was viewing the map while lying injured in the other half of the ship. The blinking red dot was getting closer and closer to his son and the only thing he could do was warn him and inform him. Finally, the mystery of the dot was revealed to be a gang of violent monkeys that ended up chasing him. Like a track star, Jaden sprinted away dodging obstacles, ducking under branches and making his way to safety. He soon outran the danger when nothing was chasing him anymore, but he did not outrun fear, as he was running from nothing. His father repeatedly told him, "Stop running, nothing is chasing you," but it was as if he had headphones on, drowning out the voice of his father while listening to the fear pumping through his ears. Finally, repeatedly, his father yelled out to him to "take a knee." He did so and calmed down. He realized that what his dad was saying was right; nothing was behind him; he was not in danger. He got a grasp of the moment and was able to continue his task.

The importance of "taking a knee" as you are chasing after your dream is important. When I first saw that scene, I thought of the importance of prayer and worship. It is a time when we stop and connect ourselves to God. We can hear His voice, receive His provision, and continue our race. As you are running towards your God-given calling, make sure you prioritize the importance of taking a knee. I encourage you to start off your mornings giving God the first fruits of your day in prayer, worship, and devotion. It is amazing how it can truly set the tone for the rest of your day and centers you in God's heart, power, and presence. I hate waking up to yelling, screaming, and drama, as it is an uphill battle from that point on. But if we learn how to practice a lifestyle of prayer and connecting our hearts with Jesus, it will be an undeniable blessing. When we take a knee, it puts our lives and situations into perspective. Fear blows things out of proportion and is challenging to get out of in the heat of the moment. Fear will tell you that a temporary inconvenience will be a permanent placement. Without taking a knee, we will spend too much time in the muck of stinking thinking, when all we need to do is jump off the crazy bus.

Matthew 6:33
"But seek first his kingdom and his righteousness, and all these things will be given to you as well."

Take the leap

I wish I could be sitting right across from you the moment you finish reading the last chapter of this book. I would ask you: What are you fighting for? And tell you many reasons why it is worth you finishing your race. Don't throw in the towel and quit a race that you haven't even started to run yet.

When I lived in North Carolina, I spent a summer doing landscaping and experienced a moment in my life that I would never forget. It was a short moment, but it created a historic life lesson. I was watering plants and bushes, standing completely still while daydreaming. I then took one step forward, when all of a sudden, a snake slithered right by my foot. I immediately discovered that the snake was there the entire time, but it started to move when I took a step forward. Maybe you feel that every time you want to start running towards your dreams, goals, and plans, something bad always happens as the enemy slithers right past you. Maybe you are waiting for the perfect moment and time before you take even baby steps towards your legacy; however, you are postponing your own breakthrough.

Make up in your mind that you aren't going to wait till Monday to get started, but take your first steps today. Just like Moses, come to the revelation that you can do the task God is calling you to do because you know who you are. You are a son and daughter of the King of Kings. Remember that it isn't possessions that grant you power, but position. Recall the truth that the Lord can use whatever you have in your life right now to get started towards your dream. Maybe you don't have all the money saved to take a full-time credit load, but can you start off reading a $3 used book from Amazon?

I have attempted to remove the blindfold you may have been wearing for years, believing that you don't have enough faith, all the while living in fear. If you can be afraid of an outcome, you can believe in a positive way for an outcome, because both faith and fear require us to believe. I hope you have had an honest conversation with yourself and have thrown away the permission slip you have been giving yourself to be lazy. Confront yourself and know for a fact that it is something you can't do rather than a task that you just won't do. Refuse to build your life on the foundation of excuses, and wonder why you crumble during storms. This may be a long road ahead of you, but it is a journey worth traveling. You have a promise and dream within you, but it is going to require a process to bring it out of you. So, as you are feeling pushed, pressed, and at times crushed in the journey, know that just like a diamond, you are being prepared to shine.

I hope you made the list of your successes and your regrets from the past so you can continue to win and end the losses. I have no doubt that you can do this, you are a winner, and you are an overcomer. My prayer is that you are no longer leaving your success up to chance. Stop living your life hoping to hit the jackpot while making the least amount of effort. Know you are going to get out what you put in. Get off your momma's couch, eating pork rinds, binge-watching TV shows while waiting for your big break. Stop treating favor like a lottery ticket and make a name for yourself in the eyes of God and man. You are destined to win, but you need to be positioned to be a winner. As wide receivers, we can blame God as the quarterback for throwing bad passes, when the fact is that we have been trying to catch what He is sending our way with our hands in our pockets and our mouths shut.

You have been giving your first name to everyone else for such a long time, but it is time that you live for your last name. There is nothing wrong with being an employee or serving another person's vision; just don't forget or forfeit your own. Your legacy is connected to your name, and your name will be the legs of the table that your kids and their kids will dine off. Whatever that goal, vision, and dream, maybe this is

> Your legacy is connected to your name, and your name will be the legs of the table that your kids and their kids will dine off.

your chance to take the leap. Don't be a daydreamer; be a "day-doer." No more excuses and no more fear. I regret that it took me thirty years to know that I am not dumb and that my dreams aren't pointless and unattainable. Don't wait that long, living in a man-made prison while the key to the lock is made out of your willingness to say yes. Show that bully of anxiety who is boss and stand up to uncertainty. You can, and you will be whom God has called you to be. Refuse to invite destiny over to your house and then ignore the knock on the door when he calls you off the comfort zone of your couch.

Knock knock! You know what, I can hear it now. Your purpose has arrived. Get up and get dressed, because this is your chance!

ABOUT THE AUTHOR

Timothy McCain is a much-sought-after international evangelist and founder of Opening Eyes Ministries. He has a heart for the lost and for stirring the embers of revival. He, his wife Madai, and son Hezekiah travel to the nations and share a message of hope birthed from their own personal experiences of pain and adversity.

With a unique approach of transparency and no-nonsense messaging, they have seen thousands make commitments to the Lord. Timothy's desire is for people to have a true encounter with the Lord that supersedes any mere religious experience. The heartbeat of this man is to chase the sinner, restore the broken, and heal the hurting.

FURTHER READING

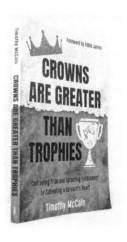

Second Chronicles, chapters 22–26, talks about the life and legacy of three kings whose reigns started out well but didn't end well. They represented three generations that fell by the same mistake and crippling character trait called entitlement. Due to their pride, they pushed away and even killed counsel and advice. They forgot about the crown they wore and the covenant that was connected to them, but gave much attention to the endeavors (trophies) that they obtained. The cycle could have been stopped, but none of the three stood up and cultivated a servant's heart to break the generational curses and patterns of behavior that were destroying their family. Will you be the one who discontinues the cycle and changes the trajectory of your family?

CPSIA information can be obtained
at www.ICGtesting.com
Printed in the USA
FFHW011406121119
56014363-61960FF

9 781545 675922